SSCI 论文写作与发表

主　编　王笑卿　石宝峰
参　编　董轶哲　陈　伟

机械工业出版社

本教材内容以当代中国社会经济发展前沿问题为基础，精选农业经济、金融风险、公司治理等方向的 25 篇社会学及经济管理学科经典 SSCI 论文为语料，以功能语言学视域下的语篇分析为主要工具，通过解析示例论文的语篇结构、句法特征及篇章功能等，帮助学习者了解 SSCI 期刊论文的体裁风格，构建高效的文献阅读和论文写作方法。

全书共分为 12 章，分为论文概述、论文主体写作、论文辅体写作及论文投稿与发表四个部分，全方位展示期刊论文写作与发表的各个环节。

本教材提供了丰富的拓展资源。通过扫描教材中的二维码，读者可以获得相关主题的拓展教学视频及 25 篇示例论文原文。本教材还在大部分教学单元设计了"学术知识小课堂"版块及配套单元练习，以期为教师课堂教学活动提供参考内容并为学习者的写作训练提供实践平台。

本教材适用于高校和科研院所人文社会学科的硕士和博士研究生，以及有英语学术写作和国际 SSCI 期刊论文发表需求的专业教师与科研人员。

图书在版编目（CIP）数据

SSCI 论文写作与发表 / 王笑卿，石宝峰主编. — 北京：机械工业出版社，2023.3（2024.12 重印）

ISBN 978-7-111-72034-8

Ⅰ.①S… Ⅱ.①王…②石… Ⅲ.①论文-写作 Ⅳ.①H152.3

中国版本图书馆 CIP 数据核字（2022）第 215862 号

机械工业出版社（北京市百万庄大街 22 号　邮政编码 100037）
策划编辑：韩效杰　　　　　责任编辑：韩效杰
责任校对：李　杉　梁　静　封面设计：王　旭
责任印制：邓　博
北京盛通数码印刷有限公司印刷
2024 年 12 月第 1 版第 4 次印刷
184mm×260mm・7.5 印张・179 千字
标准书号：ISBN 978-7-111-72034-8
定价：39.00 元

电话服务　　　　　　　　　网络服务
客服电话：010-88361066　　机　工　官　网：www.cmpbook.com
　　　　　010-88379833　　机　工　官　博：weibo.com/cmp1952
　　　　　010-68326294　　金　书　网：www.golden-book.com
封底无防伪标均为盗版　　　机工教育服务网：www.cmpedu.com

前　言

―――――――――――――――― PREFACE ――――――――――――――――

在推动"双一流"建设和高等教育国际化战略的背景下，我国高校及各级科研院所肩负着开展前沿科学研究、国际合作、技术推广等使命，因此相关人员急需具备更高水平的科研创新和学术交流能力。国际学术交流，特别是国际学术发表，是硕士、博士研究生及新入门的研究人员融入学界、发展个人学术事业的首要途径。

在当代中国社会、经济飞速发展的黄金时期，"乡村振兴""一带一路""双碳"等背景下的农村社会学、农业经济管理等领域产生了一系列原创性的研究成果，发展出了一系列具有实践创新意义的政策建议及问题解决路径。让世界听到中国声音，用规范的学术语言建立中国的学术话语权，也需要硕士、博士研究生和科研人员具备良好的交流功底与学术素养。

期刊论文的写作与发表具有"前沿性"与"规范性"并存的特征。一篇好的研究论文既要在内容上反映其学术价值，又要用简洁规范的语言将其呈现，以获得期刊编辑、审稿人和读者的青睐。因此，针对期刊论文的写作与发表教学就需要具有不同学科背景的教师各抒所长。基于"科教融合、协同育人"的编写理念，本教材的编写团队邀请了在农业经济管理、农村社会学等研究领域具有高水平科研创新能力且在国际高水平期刊连续发文的科研人员，常年在教学一线开设学术英语写作课程的英语教师，以及SSCI（社会科学引文索引）期刊的审稿人共同参与，以多元化视角为读者提供从研究选题到论文写作再到投稿发表的全方位指导。

人文社会学科的研究论文有其独特的语言风格。SSCI期刊论文的体裁及写作范式与其他科技论文存在很大差异，但目前专门针对人文社会科学方向的论文写作教材少之又少。本教材的出版就是希望能够填补现有教材市场的空白，为人文社会学科的研究者和硕士、博士研究生提供一本针对性较强的论文写作指导用书。

由于编者时间和精力有限，书中难免存在错误与不当之处，敬请广大读者批评指正。

编　者

目　录

CONTENTS

前　言

第 1 篇　SSCI 论文概述

第 1 章　走近科学问题 … 2
- 1.1　科学问题的凝练 … 2
  - 1.1.1　科学问题及其来源 … 2
  - 1.1.2　解决科学问题的思路 … 2
- 1.2　科学问题的创新 … 3
- 1.3　科学问题的解决 … 4
- 课外拓展与练习 … 5

第 2 章　SSCI 论文的基本概念 … 7
- 2.1　SSCI 论文的特点及分类 … 7
  - 2.1.1　SSCI 论文的特点 … 7
  - 2.1.2　SSCI 论文的分类 … 9
- 2.2　SSCI 论文的结构及要素 … 10
  - 2.2.1　SSCI 论文的主体及要素 … 10
  - 2.2.2　SSCI 论文的辅体及要素 … 11
- 课外拓展与练习 … 13

第 3 章　SSCI 论文的语言特点与写作风格 … 15
- 3.1　SSCI 论文的词汇使用特征 … 15
  - 3.1.1　常见词汇的学术用法 … 15
  - 3.1.2　词汇的多样性 … 16
  - 3.1.3　语块的使用策略 … 17
- 3.2　SSCI 论文中的名词化表达 … 17
- 3.3　SSCI 论文的写作风格 … 19
  - 3.3.1　SSCI 论文的表达规范 … 19
  - 3.3.2　去人称化的句法结构 … 20
- 课外拓展与练习 … 20

第 2 篇　SSCI 论文主体写作

第 4 章　引言一：研究背景与文献综述 … 26
- 4.1　引言阶段 I：介绍研究背景和主题 … 26
- 4.2　引言阶段 II：引述前人相关研究 … 28
  - 4.2.1　文献引述的组织形式 … 28

  4.2.2 文内引用的语言策略 ………………………………………………… 30
 课外拓展与练习 ……………………………………………………………………… 33

第5章 引言二：陈述现有研究

5.1 引言阶段Ⅲ：指出研究不足 ………………………………………………… 35
  5.1.1 引言阶段Ⅲ的信息要素 ………………………………………………… 35
  5.1.2 研究现状与研究不足的交替进行 ……………………………………… 37
  5.1.3 引言阶段Ⅲ的语言特征 ………………………………………………… 38
5.2 引言阶段Ⅳ：陈述研究设计（目的） ………………………………………… 38
  5.2.1 引言阶段Ⅳ的语言特征 ………………………………………………… 38
  5.2.2 研究设计（目的）与文献综述的交替进行 …………………………… 39
5.3 引言阶段Ⅴ：表明研究贡献（可选） ………………………………………… 40
  5.3.1 陈述创新的研究视角、对象或方法 …………………………………… 40
  5.3.2 陈述对现有文献的拓展 ………………………………………………… 40
  5.3.3 陈述对本领域研究的边际贡献 ………………………………………… 41
5.4 引言阶段Ⅵ：介绍论文框架（可选） ………………………………………… 41
 课外拓展与练习 ……………………………………………………………………… 42

第6章 描述研究方法

6.1 研究方法的重要性 …………………………………………………………… 44
6.2 研究方法的信息要素 ………………………………………………………… 45
6.3 研究方法的语言特征 ………………………………………………………… 46
  6.3.1 描述模型 ………………………………………………………………… 46
  6.3.2 描述数据的采集和分析 ………………………………………………… 47
 课外拓展与练习 ……………………………………………………………………… 48

第7章 叙述研究结果

7.1 研究结果文本部分的信息要素 ……………………………………………… 53
7.2 叙述研究结果的语言特征 …………………………………………………… 55
  7.2.1 叙述研究结果的句法特征 ……………………………………………… 55
  7.2.2 叙述研究结果的动词时态 ……………………………………………… 56
7.3 对研究结果的解释说明 ……………………………………………………… 57
 课外拓展与练习 ……………………………………………………………………… 59

第8章 讨论与结论

8.1 "讨论"部分的信息要素 …………………………………………………… 64
8.2 "讨论"部分的语言特征 …………………………………………………… 66
  8.2.1 "讨论"部分的句法特征 ……………………………………………… 66
  8.2.2 "讨论"部分的动词时态 ……………………………………………… 67
8.3 "讨论"部分的引用功能 …………………………………………………… 67
8.4 SSCI论文的"结论"部分 …………………………………………………… 68
 课外拓展与练习 ……………………………………………………………………… 68

第3篇 SSCI论文辅体写作

第9章 标题与摘要

9.1 摘要的撰写 …………………………………………………………………… 72

9.1.1 摘要的规范 ··· 72
9.1.2 摘要的信息要素 ·· 72
9.2 给论文一个"好"标题 ·· 73
9.2.1 标题的基本功能 ·· 74
9.2.2 标题的拟定及实例分析 ·· 74
课外拓展与练习 ··· 77

第 10 章 图表与表格 ··· 81
10.1 图表与表格的信息要素 ·· 81
10.2 图表与表格的描述 ·· 82
课外拓展与练习 ··· 83

第 4 篇 SSCI 论文投稿与发表

第 11 章 期刊选择与论文投稿 ··· 88
11.1 选择目标期刊 ··· 88
11.1.1 利用题目与关键词筛选期刊 ·· 88
11.1.2 阅读"作者指南" ··· 88
11.1.3 阅读"投稿指南与要求" ·· 89
11.2 撰写投稿信 ·· 90
11.3 准备初稿 ··· 91
课外拓展与练习 ··· 92

第 12 章 论文的修改与发表 ·· 94
12.1 SSCI 论文的"同行评议"制度 ·· 94
12.1.1 "同行评议"制度起源 ··· 94
12.1.2 期刊编辑与审稿人 ·· 94
12.2 投稿的反馈 ·· 95
12.3 论文的修改与回复 ·· 99
12.3.1 撰写回复信 ·· 99
12.3.2 呈现论文的修改 ·· 100
12.4 论文的制作与发表 ·· 101

附录 示范论文(Article Examples)列表 ································· 104

部分参考答案 ··· 106

参考文献 ··· 110

第 1 篇

SSCI论文概述

第 1 章 走近科学问题

1.1 科学问题的凝练

1.1.1 科学问题及其来源

清晰明确的科学问题是每一项科学研究的起点。好的科学问题往往来源于一个新颖的研究主题（research topic）。根据 SAGE Knowledge（社会科学领域的电子书平台）的定义："研究主题是研究者开启研究时感兴趣的方向或问题。选择、提炼一个主题是一个持续的过程，研究者通过这个过程来探索、定义和完善他们的想法。"最终，通过这个过程，研究人员将想知道的内容转化为**清晰的说明性的疑问句**，这就是科学问题，也叫研究问题（research question）。2018 年，权威学术期刊《科学》（Science）在纪念其创刊 125 周年之际，公布了全球 125 个最具挑战性的科学问题[①]。涉及经济学及社会学的经典问题如下：

- 为什么一些国家向前发展，而一些国家的发展停滞？
- 政府高额赤字对国家利益和经济增长速度有什么影响？
- 政治和经济自由密切相关吗？
- 为什么改变撒哈拉地区贫困状态的努力几乎全部失败？

这些科学问题看起来很宏大，却又与我们的生活息息相关。科研人员是如何获取并提出这些问题的？一般而言，科学问题的提出可以通过以下三种渠道实现。

（1）现实渠道

现实渠道的科学问题包括国家重大战略发展、社会经济发展或区域经济发展中需要解决的问题；通过调研、实地考察及田野观察等方式发现的科学问题。例如：在"乡村振兴"战略背景下，如何解决中国涉农小微企业面临的"融资难、融资贵"现实困境，就是农村金融研究需要解决的一个重大现实问题，从中可以凝练出许多的科学问题。

（2）文献渠道

通过阅读文献发现某一研究主题中尚未被充分探讨或充分解决的新问题。通过阅读和梳理某一研究主题的相关文献总结研究现状，发现研究不足，从而提出新的科学问题，以期对该研究主题的发展做出贡献。

（3）团队积累

一个科研团队会对某一研究主题长期持续关注。好的科研团队有合理的人员结构，保证了资深研究者对新入门的研究者的学术指导，从而确保科学研究的持续性。对于新入门的研究者来说，加入科研团队，并且在团队协作中发现科学问题，是提升自身科研能力和素养的有效方式。

1.1.2 解决科学问题的思路

解决科学问题的过程，就是寻找科学问题答案的过程。这个过程的核心就是**"创新"**——"创"就是要突破现有研究局限或改进现有研究方法，并拿出解决问题的可行方案；"新"是要通过规范研究、理论分

---

① https://www.science.org/content/resource/125-questions-exploration-and-discovery.

析和实证校验相结合，得到能够更好回答或解决科学问题的方式与途径。要实现科学问题的"创新"，就要做到以下三个"可行"。

（1）研究思路可行

思路的可行性体现在制定研究路径时，研究者要梳理与拟研究问题相关的文献，找出拟采用的研究思路与现有研究的区别，即拟研究的创新点或创新性。

（2）研究数据可行

数据可行性指支撑回答研究问题的数据是可获取的。具体体现为数据的有效来源及数据的可重复性，即可靠性。

（3）研究方法可行

选择恰当的方法开展研究并分析数据至关重要。社会科学领域研究方法众多，如调查法、文献法、实证分析法等。在开始进行研究之前，要考量何种方法适合本研究的数据收集和数据分析处理、研究资料是否充足、研究的有利和不利因素分别是什么、开展研究的成功率是多少、具有何种理论意义、应用价值或社会意义等。

1.2 科学问题的创新

科学研究的"创新性"是开展科研活动的灵魂，也是发表科研论文的基础。其内涵就是以突破或改进现有研究为目的，基于可行的研究方案，给出解决科学问题的更优方式和方法。要实现研究创新，首先要**找出拟研究科学问题与现有研究的区别**。只有存在区别，才有可能产生创新点或创新性，也就是潜在创新。图1-1展示了"研究创新"的两个维度及相互关系。

在这个四象限坐标轴中，第一象限表示"使用新方法解决新问题"。这类研究创新也叫"原始创新"，即产生了前所未有的重大科学发现、技术发明、原理性主导技术等创新成果，对人类发展和文明进步做出突出贡献的创新。"原始创新"发表的论文在所

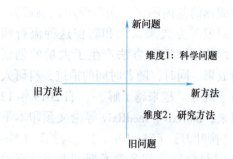

图1-1 "研究创新"维度及关系

有研究论文中所占的比重很小、甚至不到1%，但是影响力却最大。例如，2020年年初，席卷全球的新型冠状病毒肺炎（COVID-19）疫情对人们的生产生活和全球经济发展造成了巨大冲击。面对这百年不遇的重大突发公共卫生事件，如何出台与疫情防控、经济社会发展相适宜的管控政策，以及预判不同政策对经济社会发展的不同影响等研究主题就属于科学问题中的"新问题"。Duan[1]等利用中国149个行业的最新投入产出数据（2017年投入产出表），采用情景分析方法，分析了疫情形势较差（Worse Scenario, WOS）、中等（Medium Scenario, MES）和保守（Conservative Scenario, COS）三种场景对中国经济的影响。在此基础上，从财政补贴、延迟纳税或降低抵押贷款利息等方面，为政府出台中小企业融资纾困提供了对策和建议。此研究对疫情背景下解决中国中小企业融资难问题意义重大，是一项极具价值的创新研究。

第二、四象限分别表示"使用旧方法解决新问题"或者"使用新方法来解决旧问题"。这类创新分别指针对现实中出现的新问题，用传统的方式去解决它；以及针对已经存在但尚未充分解决的科学问题，随着科学技术的发展，出现了新的解决方法。

同样是为了应对"新冠全球大流行"这一"新"的公共卫生安全事件，各国研究者积极尝试采用生命科学及医学领域已经

非常成熟的基因测序、病毒作用机制研究、疫苗研发等方式来认识和防控这种流行病毒，即使用"旧"方法产生了大量的创新科研成果。同时，随着时间的推进，科研人员对于病毒"越来越了解"㊀。自 2019 年 12 月以来，bioRxiv、medRxiv 等论文预印本平台，《柳叶刀》（The Lancet）《自然》（Nature）《科学》等知名学术期刊发表的有关新型冠状病毒的论文已超过 1000 篇。今天我们再看这个问题，已经是一个"旧"问题了。但研究者对于病毒的认识还在不断加深，创新的研究方法也层出不穷。例如，新冠病毒为呼吸道病毒，鼻咽拭子采样的方法存在采样不太准确等问题，容易出现"假阳性"现象。从 2020 年 2 月中旬开始，新型冠状病毒核酸检测试剂盒检测方法获得了更多关注。这种方法检测来自鼻咽拭子、血液、肺泡灌洗液等样本中的病毒遗传物质含量，如果核酸含量超过某个临界值即为阳性结果，认为已被感染；低于某个临界值即为阴性结果，认为未被感染。这种新的检测方法进一步提高了核酸检测准确率，解决了科学研究中的"旧"问题。

上述两类研究创新在所有科研创新中分别约占 7% 的比重，同样为人类科学进步和发展做出了非常重要的贡献。

第三象限表示"使用现有方法研究已存在的问题"。虽然字面信息中并没有"新"字，但这个维度的研究创新约占到所有研究创新的 85%，是大部分科研人员，**尤其是适合新手研究者的选题领域**。如何利用已有方法来对"旧"问题进行创新研究？我们来看一个例子。

在农村金融研究中，商业银行在给不同信用等级客户贷款时，如何识别优质（信用风险等级低）客户与劣质（信用风险等级高）客户，是一个普遍存在的问题，即"旧问题"。早在 1968 年，学者 Altman[2] 在《金融学学报》（The Journal of Finance）上发文，首次利用基于线性回归的"五因素"法来评价"贷款客户"的信用风险等级。这也是定量研究"信用风险等级"的起点。在此之后，研究者开始尝试使用不同的方法来量化农村贷款客户的信用风险等级。从 20 世纪 90 年代起，在求解较为复杂的组合优化问题时，科学家提出了通过模拟自然进化过程搜索最优解的算法——"遗传算法"（由美国的 John H. Holland[3] 最早提出）解决此类问题。随着人工智能的发展，"遗传算法"已被广泛应用于组合优化、机器学习、信号处理、自适应控制和人工生命等诸多领域，发展成一种成熟的"旧"算法。近几年来，金融领域的学者们开始尝试使用"遗传算法"来解决"农村贷款的信用风险评价等级"问题，并取得了一定的成果[4]。这种"旧"方法与传统问题的"跨界"组合，就是一种"创新"。

所谓"他山之石，可以攻玉"。对于新入门的研究者来说，在开展此类研究时，要做好语言的凝练和方法的选择——让期刊编辑、审稿人、读者能够通过你的论述，了解在解决同一问题时你采用的研究方法与传统研究方法相比的优势，以及围绕拟解决的科学问题是如何将几种研究方法进行"有机组合"。

1.3　科学问题的解决

对于一个科学问题的回答，最主要的呈现方式就是**研究论文（research article）**。因此撰写高质量的研究论文以呈现研究思路和回答科学问题是研究者必备的科研素养。在研究论文中，作者需要通过论文主体的各

㊀ 彭茜，"我们分析了全球 1000 多篇新冠病毒论文，发现……"，来自新华社客户端官方账号。

个部分来呈现研究过程的三个可行性：

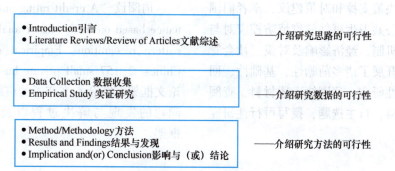

在撰写研究论文时，并不需要按照各个部分在论文中呈现的顺序依次撰写，而是应该按照研究过程发生的顺序进行撰写。建议的写作顺序如图1-2所示。

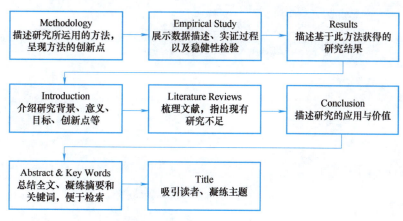

图1-2　研究论文的建议写作流程

本节课内容还可参考教学视频：

课外拓展与练习

★请完成以下练习

练习1：请以下列研究话题为基础，检索近几年的国内外文献，凝练科学问题

【话题1】

2020年是全面建成小康社会的决胜期，也是脱贫攻坚衔接乡村振兴的关键期。在经济下行压力加大、外部环境发生深刻变化的复杂形势下，坚持农业农村优先发展是打赢脱贫攻坚战，全面推进乡村振兴的总方针。优先发展农业农村、全面推进乡村振兴，是一项具有全局性和战略意义的重大任务。对中国这样一个人口大国而言，农业是基础，实现国家现代化必须实现农业现代化；对中国这样一个城乡二元结构问题依然突出的发展中国家而言，实现国家现代化必须实现农村现代化。请围绕中国农业农村经济转型发展、精准扶贫、乡村振兴战略实施过程中遇到的机遇和面临的挑战，自主选题，撰写可行性研究计划。

【话题2】

新型冠状病毒肺炎（COVID-19）疫情是一次重大突发公共卫生事件，对中国医疗卫生体系提出重大挑战，也对中国经济社会造成较大冲击。为科学防控和应对疫情等重大突发公共卫生事件、减轻其对中国经济社会的影响、完善国家治理体系和提升社会管理能力提供决策支撑和对策建议。学者们围绕重大突发公共卫生事件的疫情防控应对与管理、治理机制、经济影响及对策、社会管理等方面,开展了诸多前瞻性、基础性、回顾性和实证性研究。请围绕上述材料,查阅相关文献资料,自主选题,撰写可行性研究计划。

练习2:案例分析

请阅读"A credit rating model of microfinance based on fuzzy cluster analysis and fuzzy pattern recognition: Empirical evidence from Chinese 2,157 small private businesses"[4]的论文框架,结合本文作者的讲解,了解研究问题的发现与解决过程以及研究论文的框架。

第 2 章　SSCI 论文的基本概念

《社会科学引文索引™》（Social Sciences Citation Index™，简称 SSCI）是由美国科学信息研究所（Institute for Scientific Information，ISI）专为社会科学领域科技文献检索建立的大型数据库。其收录范围涵盖了政、史、地、文、经、哲等 58 个社会科学学科的 3400 多种期刊，是全球影响力最大、最权威的引文索引数据库之一，能反映社会科学研究最前沿的发展。SSCI 期刊论文（本书中统称 SSCI 论文）一般通过同行评议（peer-review）进行审阅与发表，以保证其数据和事实的权威性与可靠性，因此表现出独特的科学参考价值，在学术界占有重要地位。

经济管理学科期刊作为 SSCI 索引的重要来源，共包含 857 种期刊，涵盖农业经济与政策（Agricultural Economics & Policy）、商业研究（Business）、商业金融（Business & Finance）、发展研究（Development Studies）、经济学（Economics）、管理学（Management）、国际关系（International Relations）、多学科科学（Multidisciplinary Sciences）、运筹学与管理科学（Operations Research & Management Science）、城市研究（Urban Studies）共十个主要类别。（此分类依据 JCR 学科分区，截至 2021 年 6 月 30 日数据。）

2.1　SSCI 论文的特点及分类

2.1.1　SSCI 论文的特点

（1）原创性（Originality）

在人类认识和改造世界的过程中，许多重要的发现与发明都是首先通过科研发表的形式为人们所熟知。例如，1953 年，沃森和克里克建立了 DNA 双螺旋模型，使遗传领域的研究深入到分子层次，揭开了现代分子生物学的序幕。这项研究成果最早公之于世，就发表在同年的《自然》⊖ 期刊上。

同在 20 世纪 50 年代，由芝加哥大学马科维茨（Markowitz）教授提出的投资组合理论发表在金融领域顶级期刊《金融学学报》上。在他的学术论文《资产选择：有效的多样化》⊖ 中，马科维茨首次将数学中的均值和方差引入资产组合报酬的期望值去刻画组合的收益，明确定义了投资者偏好；并将边际分析原理运用于资产组合的研究分析。这一研究成果可以帮助家庭和公司合理组合其资金进行投资以实现单位风险收益最大化，对华尔街乃至全球金融发展产生了深远的影响。鉴于马科维茨教授的突出贡献，他与威廉夏普、默顿米勒三人共同获得了 1990 年的诺贝尔经济学奖。

原创性意味着 SSCI 论文呈现的研究结果是基于研究者创新的研究思想或研究路

⊖ WATSON, J., CRICK, F. Genetical Implications of the Structure of Deoxyribonucleic Acid［J］. Nature. 1953, 171, pp. 964-967.

⊖ Markowitz, H. Portfolio Selection［J］. Journal of Finance. 1952, 7, pp. 77-91.

径，为本领域贡献了新的认知。SSCI 期刊非常重视所发表研究工作的原创性。

（2）新颖性（Novelty）

不是所有的科学研究都能实现重大的发现发明或理论突破，但必须实现创新，即新颖性。新颖性是衡量科学研究价值的重要标准。为了在研究领域找到创新之处，在提出研究问题时，学者们应进行全面的文献回顾，找出该领域已知之处和需要继续探索的方向之间的差距。可能有一些领域或方向已经被研究过，但不同研究者得出的结论存在差异或矛盾，解决这些差异和矛盾，也是创新的一种途径。还有很多时候，一项研究的新颖之处就在于反驳人们已经知道的。

实现研究的新颖性，在很大程度上取决于研究者对本领域研究的深入了解程度。随着研究产出增加，许多影响力大的期刊越来越看重研究的新颖性。

（3）可读性（Readability）

国际科学界有一句名言"一项科学研究，直到其成果发表并被理解才算完成"。清晰准确地呈现科研成果是科学进程的一个基本部分，既有助于知识的传播，又有助于成果的可重复性。好的 SSCI 论文必须保证期刊编辑和审稿人在有限的时间内发现其价值，同时又能使读者在最短的时间内获得最有效的科学信息。要实现这两点，论文作者必须从论文的逻辑、语言、格式等方面提高论文的可读性。

SSCI 期刊会在投稿指南（submission guidelines）中对投稿论文从以上三个方面提出具体要求。下面，以《营销科学》（Marketing Science）期刊的投稿指南[1]为例，该期刊对"写作目标（manuscript objectives）"的描述见表 2-1。

表 2-1 《营销科学》期刊的写作目标

目　标	具体描述
Develop a Normative Theory （发展一项规范理论）	You develop a theory that provides conditions when apparently inferior alternatives are shown to be optimal. This type of research requires a high level of rigor and logic
Develop New Normative Tools （开发新的规范工具）	You should compare your tool to existing tools and show that your tool (at least under some conditions) outperforms existing tools on common measures of performance
Discover an Empirical Regularity （发现新的实证规律）	You discover an empirical regularity or discover that some published findings seem to generalize across a wide variety of situations. It is also useful to explore the implications for marketing and explore whether the research suggests new previously unknown actions
New Method Development （发展新的方法）	You develop a new method that allows better decisions or extraction of information that ultimately produces better decisions. The new method should lead (hopefully) to firms taking better actions than existing methods
Propose New Descriptive or Positive Theories （提出新的描述性理论或实证理论）	You develop a new explanation for an existing and observed phenomenon. If there are existing explanations, you provide proof that your explanation has more explanatory power. Positive theories must be testable (i. e., have refutable implications)

---

[1] https://pubsonline.informs.org/page/mksc/submission-guidelines.

(续)

目 标	具 体 描 述
Substantive Empirical Comparisons（实质性经验比较）	You compare more successful companies with less successful companies and make conclusions. This type of research requires you to pay careful attention to the quality of your data, the rigor of your analysis and the validation of your results
Theory Testing（理论测试）	You test either an existing theory or a new theory. This type of research requires you to develop competing implications for the different theories and show that your theory explains or predicts better than alternative theories
Exposition（阐述及说明）	Good ideas are often simple. When you prepare a paper for submission, please try to make it as readable as possible to as broad an audience as is feasible. The easier it is for reviewers and editors to read your paper, the more likely they are to recognize your contributions

虽然每种期刊的具体投稿要求和写作目标存在差异，但从上表的描述可以看出，SSCI 期刊对其投稿的文章总体要求体现了原创性、创新性与可读性的统一。

2.1.2 SSCI 论文的分类

SSCI 论文包含原创论文、综述论文、书评、短篇报道、个案研究等不同的形式。此处介绍经济管理学科最常见的两种论文类型。

（1）原创论文（Original Articles）

原创论文又名 original/regular research 或 research article，是 SSCI 期刊最常呈现的论文形式，用于报告一项完整的研究。原创论文包括完整的论文主体部分，篇幅一般为 7000~10000，但也因期刊与学科不同存在很大差异。原创论文中所提供的数据及研究过程描述叫作一级文献（primary literature/sources）。

（2）综述论文（Review Articles）

综述论文通过对已发表文献的述评，全面总结关于某一研究主题的研究现状，为本领域的研究前景提供视角。综述论文一般分为一般性综述（general reviews）、系统性综述（systematic reviews）和元分析（meta-analyses）。

根据期刊和研究领域，综述论文的篇幅差异也很大。对于一般性综述，篇幅为 8000~40000 字不等，而系统性综述通常少于 10000 字。也有一些期刊发表短综述，篇幅在 3000~5000 字之间。

但是，综述论文一般不适合由研究新手撰写和发表，Springer 网站对综述论文撰写的提示：

> Tip: Reviews are often written by leaders in a particular discipline after an invitation from the editors of a journal. If you would like to write a Review but have not been invited by a journal, be sure to check the journal website as some journals to not consider unsolicited Reviews. If the website does not mention whether Reviews are commissioned it is wise to send a pre-submission enquiry letter to the journal editor to propose your Review manuscript before you spend time writing it.

综述论文一般是在某一研究领域中有影响力的研究者受邀为期刊撰写的。由于这类论文不包含原创研究及新的数据，其呈现的信息和资源叫二级文献（secondary literature/sources）。

2.2 SSCI 论文的结构及要素

为了便于读者在论文的各个部分快速获取有效信息，现代 SSCI 论文的结构及要素要遵循美国国家标准研究所（American National Standards Institute）于 1972 年制定的论文结构标准，包含 Introduction（简介）、Materials and Methods（材料与方法）、Results（结果）、Discussion（讨论）和 Conclusion（结论）。

但是，Braine[5]指出，研究论文，包括 SSCI 论文的结构在学科与学科之间、期刊与期刊之间，甚至研究与研究之间，都存在差异。例如，同为管理学科下的商业研究与农村金融研究，收集数据和解决问题的路径就不尽相同。本节将探讨 SSCI 论文的主体结构要素及其变体，并对论文辅体部分的信息要素做简要介绍。

2.2.1 SSCI 论文的主体及要素

虽然学科之间及期刊要求之间存在差异，但 SSCI 论文都遵循规范化的数据呈现方式和写作风格。论文的主体结构相对固定，每个部分的信息要素及体裁范式也有一定的规范。本节先简要介绍论文的宏观框架。在经济管理学科中，一篇 SSCI 论文的主体部分包含的要素见表 2-2。

表 2-2 SSCI 论文主体的基本结构要素

Introduction	引言
Theoretical Model/Background/Framework	理论模型/背景/框架（可选）
Research Design and Data	研究设计与数据收集
Empirical Analysis/Interpretation	实证分析/解读
Results	研究结果
Discussion（s）	讨论（可选）
Conclusion and Future Implications	结论与展望

（1）经典论文框架——IMRDC 结构

现代 SSCI 论文主体的宏观框架，最常见的结构就是 IMRDC。图 2-1 展示了该框架下各部分信息要素的名称及其功能。根据 Weissberg & Bucker[6]和 Cargill & O'Connor[7]对论文篇章功能的分析，SSCI 论文的引言（Introduction）及讨论（Discussion）部分均有信息呈现的层级特征，因此用了倒梯形及正梯形对其信息呈现的特点进行描绘。

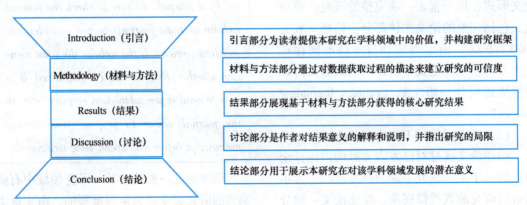

Weissberg & Bucker(1990), Cargill & O'Connor(2009)

图 2-1 SSCI 论文经典框架 IMRDC 结构

例子可看 2021 年发表在《农业经济学》(Agricultural Economics)期刊上的一篇论文主体部分的结构（AE 1[⊖]）。

（2）SSCI 论文框架及其变体——IBC 结构

但是，也有很大一部分 SSCI 论文的主体部分并不严格遵循 IMRDC 结构，而是以更详细的步骤描述研究和数据收集，见表 2-2。这种论文的框架以 IBC 结构进行呈现如图 2-2 所示。

IBC 结构基本概括了 SSCI 论文框架的主要特征，其中主体（Body）部分的信息要素会根据具体研究方向及期刊的要求存在很大的差异。

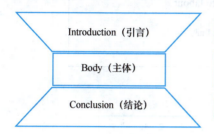

引言部分为读者提供本研究在学科领域中的价值，并构建研究框架

主体部分包含理论背景、建模、数据收集以及结果和讨论的组合，各部分使用独立标题及副标题描述研究阶段及内容

结论用于回顾本研究的主要成果并展望本研究的前景

图 2-2　SSCI 论文框架的 IBC 结构

例子可看 2021 年发表在《发展经济学学报》(Journal of Development Economics)上的一篇论文主体部分的结构（AE 18）。

2.2.2　SSCI 论文的辅体及要素

（1）署名（Author and Affiliation）

多数 SSCI 论文是由研究团队成员合作完成的。在确定论文作者顺序时，第一作者（first author）是论文最主要的贡献者，负责或监督数据收集、分析、陈述和解释结果，并将其他作者完成的论文各部分进行整合，进行最终的提交。通讯作者（corresponding author）可以是第一作者，也可以是该研究团队中的资深研究者。论文发表后，读者想要就本研究与作者沟通时，一般会联系通讯作者。其他作者按照贡献大小顺序进行排名。当然，作者的排名顺序可能因学科和期刊要求而存在差异。SSCI 论文的署名示例如图 2-3 所示。

（2）摘要（Abstract）

摘要的核心目的之一是提供检索（indexing），一般包含本研究的目的、方法和主要结果，并包含若干个关键词（key words）。确保当读者通过搜索引擎或文献数据库对某一领域的论文进行文献检索时，能够通过摘要及关键词找到相关文章。

摘要的核心目的之二是吸引读者。通过简短的一段文字，让读者快速了解论文的精髓，以便决定是否阅读全文。

（3）参考文献（Reference）

有些期刊也将这部分命名为"Bibliography"。参考文献主要列出本文中引用的事实、数据、观点等的来源，一般包含期刊论文、书籍、网页信息等。对于 SSCI 期刊来说，参考文献的信息排列必须符合要求，目前最主流的两种参考文献格式为 APA（美国心理学协会）格式和 MLA（现代语言协会）格式，具体信息可以在 https：//apastyle.apa.org/和 https：//style.mla.org/formatting-papers/ 找到。

[⊖] AE：Article Example（文章示范），本书中所有文章示范都出自已发表的 SSCI 论文，均以 AE+（1，2，3…）表示，读者可在本书附录中查看论文信息。

例2.1

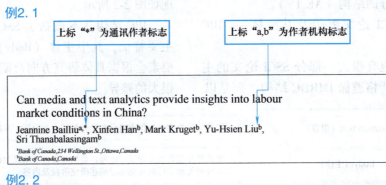

例2.2

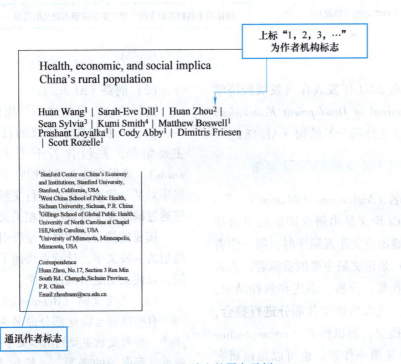

图 2-3 SSCI 论文的署名示例

（4）作者贡献（Author Contribution）

这个部分是对完成该论文的每位作者工作的具体描述，一般有以下五种描述：

1）构思和设计分析或实验（Conceived and designed the analysis/experiment）；

2）收集数据/开展实验（Collected the data/performed the experiment）；

3）提供数据或分析工具（Contributed data or analysis tools）；

4）进行数据分析或开展实验（Performed the analysis/experiment）；

5）撰写论文（Wrote the paper）。

其他论文辅体见表 2-3。

表2-3　SSCI论文辅体的要素及内容

英文名称	中文名称	主要内容
Conflict of Interest	利益冲突	作者应该阐明个人利益冲突，如与咨询机构的关系、聘雇信息、参与游说团体、拥有的股票或股份，以及任何跟基金相关的信息、费用、薪酬、报销和任何已注册的专利等； 也该披露单位利益冲突，如作者的雇主针对论文中讨论的物件或材料有任何财务利益或冲突； 如果没有任何利益冲突，表达为"No potential conflict of interest was reported by the authors"
Acknowledgements	致谢	应致谢所有不符合署名资格，但对本研究进程及文章发表过程做出贡献的个人、团体及机构，如提供咨询建议的人，资金提供者，文章校对者等
Ethical approval	道德审批	如果研究牵涉到人体或动物，或论文里面含有病例报告等，正文结束后作者一定要提供获得审批的道德审核单位或机构审查委员会名称以及核准编号，以示本研究符合道德规范。 例如：This study was approved by the Stanford University Institutional Review Board (protocol No. ***). All participants provided informed verbal consent for this study
Funding	基金来源	说明支持该研究工作的所有基金来源，列出基金单位名称与基金编号。还要说明其在研究设计、数据收集、分析和阐释，以及论文写作中的作用

课外拓展与练习

★ 学术知识小课堂

一级文献和二级文献

一、一级文献

一级文献是以作者本人的研究成果为依据而创作的原始文献或信息来源。不同学科一级文献的例子如下：

历史学：埃及卢克索神庙上的象形文字；
　　　　中国某一朝代的石刻；
　　　　十九世纪农民的手写遗嘱；
社会学：乡村调查中使用的问卷；
物理学：来自月球的岩石；
生物学：大猩猩的血液样本；
心理学：在调查个人创伤后应激障碍时的笔记。

二、二级文献

二级文献是指来自其他研究人员的二手信息和评论。主要产生于对一级文献的描述、解释与合成。SSCI论文中涉及二级文献的文章类型主要有综述论文（review articles），尤指系统性综述与元分析；书评（book criticism）；文章评论（editorial）。

对同一信息来源中一级文献与二级文献形式的比较见表2-4。

表2-4　一级文献与二级文献的比较

一 级 文 献	二 级 文 献
Novel（小说）	Articles analyzing the novel（分析该小说的论文）
Painting（绘画）	Exhibition catalog explaining the painting（画展目录）
Letters and diaries written by a historical figure（历史人物的书信与日记）	Biography of the historical figure（历史人物传记）

(续)

一级文献	二级文献
Essay by a philosopher （哲学家的文章）	Textbook summarizing the philosopher's ideas （总结该哲学家思想的教科书）
Photographs of a historical event （某一历史事件的照片）	Documentary about the historical event （某一历史事件的纪录片）
Government documents about a new policy （政府有关新政的文件）	Newspaper article about the new policy （关于政府新政的新闻报道）
Results of an opinion poll （民意调查结果）	Blog post interpreting the results of the poll （对民意调查结果的博文解读）
Empirical study （实证研究）	Literature review that cites the study （引用某一实证研究的文献综述）

★ 请完成以下练习

练习1：判断下列资源是一级文献还是二级文献

1. Documentaries

（1）If you are researching the filmmaking techniques used in historical documentaries, the documentary is a **Primary**（ ）**Secondary**（ ）source.

（2）If you are researching the causes of World War I, a recent documentary about the war is a **Primary**（ ）**Secondary**（ ）source.

2. Reviews and Essays

（1）Your paper is about the novels of Ernest Hemingway, a magazine review of one of his novels is a **Primary**（ ）**Secondary**（ ）source.

（2）Your paper is about the critical reception of Toni Morrison's work, a magazine review of one of her novels is a **Primary**（ ）**Secondary**（ ）source.

3. Newspaper Articles

（1）If your aim is to analyze the government's economic policy, a newspaper article about a new policy is a **Primary**（ ）**Secondary**（ ）source.

（2）If your aim is to analyze media coverage of economic issues, the newspaper article is a **Primary**（ ）**Secondary**（ ）source.

练习2：语篇分析

请从你感兴趣的研究领域选择相应的SSCI期刊2~3种，观察近期该刊发表的文章类型，并对其从以下方面进行比较，完成以下表格。

Classifications （SSCI论文分类）	Length （篇幅）	Paradigm/Novelty （规范性/创新性）	Primary/Secondary Literature （一级文献/二级文献）
Original Article	Short ○ Long ○	Yes ○ No ○	Primary ○ Secondary ○
Review	Short ○ Long ○	Yes ○ No ○	Primary ○ Secondary ○
Brief communications	Short ○ Long ○	Yes ○ No ○	Primary ○ Secondary ○
Others	Short ○ Long ○	Yes ○ No ○	Primary ○ Secondary ○

第3章 SSCI论文的语言特点与写作风格

对EAL①(二语)学习者而言,在撰写论文之前,应首先熟悉并掌握SSCI论文的语言特征和写作风格。SSCI论文遵循科技写作的体裁风格,总体上简洁、规范但又表达严谨。要实现这些目标,作者在撰写论文之前,已经在头脑中构思好了自己写作的方式和使用的语言。接下来,本章将对SSCI论文在写作风格上的共性特点进行总结。对读者而言,了解论文写作风格,能更好地理解科学语言的表达规范,快速适应本学科作者的表达习惯,提高文献阅读和写作效率。

3.1 SSCI论文的词汇使用特征

对本领域学术词汇和专业词汇的掌握和理解程度在很大程度上影响他们对文章的理解程度。下面,我们就SSCI论文中词汇的使用特征进行总结。

3.1.1 常见词汇的学术用法

SSCI论文中包含很多在通用语境中也会使用的词汇,但是意思却不尽相同。只有掌握这些词汇的学术用法,才不至于在理解文章时产生歧义。

例如:

- When we consider separately rural and urban **branches** per capita, we similarly find that higher branch **penetration** in 1960 is associated with fewer additional rural branches during the period of rural branching operation.

此句中,**branch**(a part of a government or other large organization that deals with one particular aspect of its work)是指大型机构的"分支机构"。penetrate(go into or through, see through)本意为"进入、穿透或看透",在金融领域,**penetration** 表示"渗透率"。

- To control the possible endogeneity problem, we have applied pooled OLS, first difference GMM, system GMM and IV regressions in the **robustness** test.

此句中,robust(strong, not likely to be weak)本意为"强健的、坚固的",在统计学或计量经济学中,常见的"robustness test"表示采用计量统计方法进行稳定性检验,译为"稳健性检验"或"鲁棒性测试"。

- It is widely recognized that the **credit spread** reflects not only a **default premium** determined by the firm's credit risk, but also a **liquidity premium** due to the illiquidity of the **secondary debt market**.

此句中涉及了众多金融学专有词汇:信用价差(Credit Spread)、违约溢价(Default Premium)、流动性溢价(Liquidity Premium)、二级债务市场(Secondary Debt Market)等。

试比较下列词汇的不同用法,见表3-1。

---

① EAL: English as Additional Language.

表 3-1 不同语境下的词汇含义比较

词汇	通用语境	金融语境	保险语境
Spread（n.）	increase（扩展，蔓延） variety（广泛，多样） area covered（所占区域）	the difference between two rates or prices （差额，差幅）	
default	n. failure to do（违约） adj. being not change（原样）	failure to do （违约）	
Premium（n.）	adj. of high quality （多为形容词性）（高昂的，优质的）	an extra payment added to the basic amount（溢价）	money pay for an insurance（保险费）

3.1.2 词汇的多样性

词汇的多样性（lexical variation）是指在一篇论文中使用不同形式的词汇来表达相同或相似的意思。SSCI 论文的语言使用体现出了词汇的多样性的特点。

例 3.1（AE 2）

Eco-innovation can bring <u>performance improvements</u>, but related conditions are needed to enable the processes for achieving the <u>desired performance outcomes</u>. In operations management, researchers have advanced from investigations on management practices to examine contextual conditions for explaining <u>success</u> among enterprises (Sousa and Voss, 2008). Thus, contingency factors have been studied concerning how environmental management practices can lead to <u>performance gains</u> (Alves et al., 2017; Wiengarten et al., 2012).

例 3.1 中描述生态创新（eco-innovation）对绩效提升（performance improvement）的作用。下画线标出部分的信息均表达"绩效提升或改进"这一概念。可以看出，这些表达的形式虽略有差异，但却传达了相同的意思，体现了作者在写作过程中对词汇多样性的运用。

例 3.2（AE 4）

It is found that China's aggregate aid has <u>a positive impact</u> on GDP growth in African countries, while ODI <u>does not have a significant impact</u> on the GDP growth rate. In addition, natural resources, openness and aid from OECD countries <u>all positively affect</u> GDP growth.

例 3.2 中分别描述三个变量对"GDP 增速（GDP growth）"的影响，描述"影响"时作者使用的不同表达见表 3-2。

表 3-2 一篇论文中对"影响"含义的不同表达

要素 1	是/否产生积极影响	要素 2
China's aggregate aid（中国援助总额）	has a positive impact on	
ODI（Overseas Direct Investment）（海外直接投资）	does not have a significant impact on	GDP Growth （GDP 增速）
Natural resources, openness and aid from OECD countries （经合组织国家的自然资源、开放程度及援助）	all positively affect	

提高 SSCI 论文语言质量的一个重要方面就是在词汇层面实现表达多样化。通过上述例子可以看出，这种多样化不仅体现在用不同的词表达相同的意思，也可以通过对原

词汇进行缩略或扩展实现。例子见表 3-3。

表 3-3 一篇论文中对"经济学家"和"文献"的不同表达

经济学家	文献
Economists	Literature
The economics professional	Papers and reports
Experts in the economic study	The publication of papers and reports

3.1.3 语块的使用策略

语块（lexical chunks）是按照学术语言的惯用规则生成的语言单位。在使用这些语言单位时，使用者并不需要有意识地关注其语法结构，因此大大缩短了从理解到产出语言信息的时间。在 SSCI 论文写作这种适用于全球读者且高效的语言使用场景下，训练有素的作者在表达特定信息时会倾向选择本领域适用的、预先编制好的语块来呈现信息。Lewis[8]将语块分成四种类型：一是单词和聚合词，通常指 2~3 个词组成的固定短语，不可变化，不可分割；二是搭配词，指出现频率很高的单词组合；三是固定表达，指形式固定且具有广泛语用功能的交际套语、谚语等；四是半固定表达，通常指非连续的结构性短语。例如，

• Although issues have been raised with respect to many of China's official statistics, those pertaining to the labor market are seen as particularly problematic.（about, relevant to）

• The methodology that we use in this paper builds on that of Tobback et al.（2018）who employ a supervised machine learning technique to develop an economic policy uncertainty index for Belgium.（to use a skill, method, etc. for a particular purpose）

• We drew on Antenucci et al.（2014）and translated the keywords into Chinese.（to use a helpful resource）

• All the results in Table 5 are consistent with Table 4, and hence our results are robust when applying different empirical methodologies.（agree with, be the same as）

在论文写作中恰当地、熟练地运用语块会增强信息传递效率，优化写作风格。

3.2 SSCI 论文中的名词化表达

科技语言的表达优先考虑的是行动，大多数情况下不强调对行动负责的人。因此，将动词、形容词及其他名词短语等进行名词化（nominalization），是 SSCI 论文写作的一个明显特征。下面，我们通过一组科技新闻报道与 SSCI 论文写作对比来理解"名词化"这一语言特征的应用。

2021 年，中国科学院预测科学研究中心、第三世界科学院汪寿阳院士团队在《自然·通讯》（*Nature Communications*）期刊上发表一篇评估"中国比特币区块链运营对碳排放和可持续发展影响"的论文。其研究工作被英美多家主流新闻媒体报道。我们通过比较著名财经媒体"福布斯（Forbes）"的报道与该论文摘要部分对应的描述来看两种体裁在传达同一信息时的语言差异见表 3-4。

表 3-4 科技论文中名词短语的使用示例

新闻报道语境	科研论文语境
Forbes	nature COMMUNICATIONS

(续)

新闻报道语境	科研论文语境
Bitcoin Could Churn Out 130 Million Tons Of Carbon, Undermining Climate Action. Here's One Way To Tackle That 标题：比特币可能产生1.3亿吨碳排放，破坏全球气候行动。这里有一种方法来解决这个问题	Policy assessments for the carbon emission flows and sustainability of Bitcoin blockchain operation in China 标题：对中国比特币区块链操作的碳排放流量及可持续发展的政策评估
The power demands and carbon emissions of bitcoin mining could undermine global efforts to combat climate change if stringent regulations are not placed upon the industry, a Chinese study has found By 2024, mining of the cryptocurrency in China alone could use as much power as the entire nation of Italy uses in a year, with greenhouse gas emissions equaling those of the Czech Republic	We find that without any policy interventions, the annual energy consumption of the Bitcoin blockchain in China is expected to peak in 2024 at 296.59 Twh Internationally, this emission output would exceed the total annualized greenhouse gas emission output of the Czech Republic and Qatar
基于中国数据研究发现，如果对比特币挖矿不实行严格监管，比特币挖矿机的电力需求和碳排放可能会破坏全球应对气候变化的努力 到2024年，仅在中国挖掘加密货币，其用电量将相当于意大利全国一年内的电力使用，温室气体排放量相当于捷克共和国一年的排放量	研究发现，没有任何干预政策，中国比特币区块链的年均能源消耗预计将在2024年达到峰值——296.59太瓦时（Twh）。通过国际对比不难看出，此排放量超出捷克共和国与卡塔尔两国年均温室气体排放量总和

从表3-4中的例子可以看出，在传达同样的信息时，由于目标读者不同，科技论文呈现的信息更加具体和专业。这种具体性和专业性体现在语言**名词化**的使用上。科技语言的这一"名词化特征"，可以实现两个目标：

（1）简化句子结构，更直接地体现两个变量之间的关系。来看下面的例子：

1）Radiation was accidentally released over a 24-hour period, damaging a wide area for a long time.

2）Accidental release of radiation over a 24-hour period caused widespread long-term damage.

很明显，2）句比1）句更接近于科技论文使用的语言。与1）相比，2）句将两个信息要素"radiation"和"damage"名词化，使用"radiation" **caused** "damage"，将两个变量的关系更直接地呈现。

（2）便于检索（retrieve）。以名词词组形式呈现研究对象、方法及研究过程等，能够在摘要中充分体现研究的目标、方法、重要结果及研究意义如图3-1所示。同时，能够更好地提炼论文的关键词，便于检索——让目标读者在海量信息中能够快速找到相关论文，同时提高论文的被引率。

ARTICLE INFO

Keywords:
Eco-innovation
Performance
Manufacturing
Small and medium-sized manufacturing enterprise
Contingency theory

ABSTRACT

Due to the growing public quest for environmental protection, small and medium-sized manufacturing enterprises (SMMEs) are under pressure to adopt eco-innovation to improve their operations. However, whether and how eco-innovation efforts can bring performance improvements may rely on the implementation level of eco-innovation and other traditional environmental management (TEM) practices. Drawing on the contingency theory, we develop and empirically test a model which proposes the existence of different firm clusters of SMMEs based on their eco-innovation implementation levels and that the performance improvement associated with eco-innovation practices is contingent on the firm clusters and TEM practices (i.e., internal source reduction, external compliance and communication, and internal management and control). Using survey data collected from 382 SMMEs in China, our cluster analytic results reveal two firm clusters of SMMEs characterized by three types of eco-innovation (technology, management, and marketing) implementation. From the results, we observed eco-innovation adopters involving 225 SMMEs (58.9% of the sample). The rest of 157 SMMEs (41.1% of the sample) are labeled as eco-innovation planners. T-test results show that the implementation levels of eco-innovation and TEM practices, as well as environmental and economic performance improvements, are different between eco-innovation planners and adopters. Results from hierarchical regression analyses further show that implementing certain eco-innovation practices jointly with TEM practices is beneficial for performance improvements. External compliance and communication are helpful for management innovation to bring environmental performance among eco-innovation planners, but it can be detrimental to environmental image together with marketing innovation. For eco-innovation adopters, internal source reduction is helpful for both technology and management innovation to deliver environmental performance. Technology innovation and internal source reduction can jointly bring economic performance improvement among eco-innovation planners, but such joint efforts can weaken the economic performance improvement for eco-innovation adopters. Our paper contributes knowledge on the role of eco-innovation to bring performance gains among SMMEs in China, a major manufacturing hub in Asia servicing global production demands. We also examine the performance contingencies of eco-innovation with TEM practices in the SMMEs, providing practical implications for them to improve operations, as well as policy insights for governments to promote the performance benefits of eco-innovation, particularly targeting for the smaller-sized manufacturers in the industry.

图 3-1　SSCI 论文关键词在摘要中位置示例（AE 21）

3.3　SSCI 论文的写作风格

3.3.1　SSCI 论文的表达规范

蔡基刚[9]总结了 SSCI 论文写作中语言表达的规范（p. 164）。此处，根据 SSCI 论文在写作上呈现的一些特点，用表 3-5 对具体细节规范进行说明。

从表 3-5 中的一些细节，我们可以看出 SSCI 论文的写作风格与日常写作及其他正式写作文体有很多不同之处。需要读者在阅读和写作中不断地总结与积累。

表 3-5　SSCI 论文的表达规范

1	使用学术词汇如 offspring，manager 而不是用口语词汇如 kids，boss
2	描述变化或结果时使用名词短语，如 a dramatic increase；a satisfactory result。避免使用 get better，get worse 等非正式表达
3	在对信息否定时，使用正式的否定词：no，few，little。避免使用 not... any，not... much/many
4	避免使用问句。如 How can we engage students in learning? 可以说 There are several practical strategies to engage students in learning
5	避免在句首使用连接词，如 and，but，also，so。使用相对正式的连词如 Thus，Yet，In addition 等
6	避免使用表示绝对程度的词，如 all，none，best 等。可以使用更客观精确的表达，如 a minimal extent，the lowest level，a significant proportion
7	在文中必要处使用“引用”来增加信息的可靠性
8	在陈述时使用 might，may，seem，probably 等表确定程度的词
9	避免在句首使用 actually，generally 等词，可以把这些词放在句中
10	避免使用第二人称 you 或 your（s）
11	避免使用 Can't，it's，don't 等缩写，使用完整形式：cannot，it is，Do not

(续)

12	在描述信息时避免使用模糊的代词，如 nothing or something，可以替换为 factor, issue 等
13	避免在句末使用 and so on, etc. 等词，可用具体信息结尾。试比较： There are many causes of student exhaustion, such as poor diet, part-time work and so on. There are many causes of student exhaustion, such as poor diet, part-time work and stress

3.3.2 去人称化的句法结构

科技写作的特征之一是突出信息，弱化人称。因此包括 SSCI 论文写作在内的科技体裁都倾向使用去人称化的句法结构（impersonal syntax structure）来实现这一目标。我们将 SSCI 论文中这些具体的句法特征进行分类，总结见表 3-6。

表 3-6　SSCI 论文中去人称化句法结构分类

句法结构名称	举　例
"被动"结构 The Passive Structure	The first two indicators <u>are usually measured by</u> the proportion of GDP. Once the TFIDF matrix <u>is constructed</u>, it can be used as an input into the SVM algorithm. In this type of rule, a central bank <u>is assumed to</u> conduct monetary policy by responding to deviations in GDP growth from its target and to other additional relevant variables
"There be+名词"结构 There be + N	Financial depth relates to the overall extent of financial services available in a country and <u>there is an extensive literature</u> documenting the importance of depth for growth and poverty alleviation. <u>There are concerns that</u> these measures may have slowed economic growth and created substantial consequences for individual livelihoods（Brodzicki, 2020）
"It +被动语态+that"结构 It be+Ved that	<u>It can be clearly seen that</u> public banks dominate the banking sector of India by sizing about 68% of branches and about 70% of total credit. <u>It is evidently proved that</u> chains enter big cities earlier than the small cities, on average

在了解这些句法结构之后，读者会在任何一篇 SSCI 论文中找到这些结构的存在。无论作者选择何种形式的去人称化结构，目的都在于客观呈现信息本身，弱化由作者主观观点对读者产生的影响，体现科技语言规范严谨的特点。

课外拓展与练习

★学术知识小课堂

主动语态与被动语态

一、写作中的主动与被动（Active and Passive Verbs in Science Writing）

英语中动词语态的用法，相信大家并不陌生。主动还是被动，主要取决于动作发出者与施动对象的位置，如图 3-2 所示。

在论文写作中，论文各个部分使用的动词语态也不一样。请看以下例文（AE 10）：

Introduction

In order to improve its ecological environment, the state <u>has implemented</u> a series of vegetation restoration projects since 1998（Yin, 2010; Qu et al., 2018; Yin et al., 2018）, including the Returning Farmland to Forest and Grass Program（RFFG）, which <u>has attracted</u> worldwide attention. The pilot implementation of the RFFG <u>has been implemented</u> in individual counties in China（Tang, 2004）. Although RFFG literally involves only the conversion of cultivated land to forest and grassland, other related measures, such as the Forest Land Conservation（FLC）and the Grass Land Conservation（GLC）<u>are combined</u> in the meantime（Zhang et al., 2018a, 2019a）. Overall, eco-

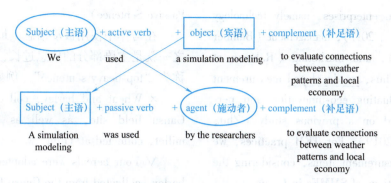

图 3-2 主动语态与被动语态的句子结构

logical projects <u>have achieved</u> remarkable results (FAO, 2000) and vegetation <u>has been significantly restored</u>.

Materials and Methods

The socio-economic data <u>were mainly extracted</u> from the land use maps interpreted from the TM images and annual socio-economic statistics from 1999 to 2010, and they <u>were taken</u> average values in these years then. The vegetation index data set <u>is derived</u> from the 16-day MOD13Q1 data product provided by the LPDAAC (Land Process Distributed Active Archive Center), with a resolution of 250 m × 250 m. Considering the time lag of vegetation growth relative to land-use type adjustment, the time nodes of the vegetation index data <u>are identified as</u> 2000 and 2011 respectively, and the final used yearly vegetation data <u>were synthesized</u> with all 16-day MOD13Q1 data in a certain year according to the average vegetation index value of the growing season (Zhang et al., 2018a).

在"引言"部分,作者需要将观点与事实相结合,因此这部分既有主动语态,也有被动语态。"材料与方法"部分重在描述过程,无须强调研究者本人的身份,因此多用被动语态。

二、语态的选择(Active or Passive Voice?)

在写作中,尤其是在研究方法部分,我们到底该不该使用被动语态呢?这里分享两个判断标准如下:

标准1:论文的目标读者是否需要知道动作的发出者?

如果是谁发出了这个动作对读者来说不重要,这样的信息就可以考虑使用被动语态。

× The researchers collected data from all sites biweekly.

√ Data were collected from all sites biweekly.

标准2:虽然对于科技写作来讲,在客观陈述"过程""事实"等信息时,多使用被动语态。但具体的语言使用规范还是要看投稿期刊的语言风格。

例如,发表在 *International Journal of Production Economics* 这个期刊上的这篇文章,在方法部分描述数据收集过程时,就全部使用第一人称"we"引导的主动语态。这种用法可能与期刊要求的语言风格有关,是作者投稿这个期刊时,要注意的地方。请看以下例文(AE 21):

Methodology

Items development and data collection

Learning from Reger (2003) who introduced innovation for strategic competence and a previous study on innovation for firms' competitiveness (Hwang, 2004), <u>we included</u> three implementation dimensions for evaluating innovation implementation in enterprises, namely technology (Bocquet et al., 2017), management (Bamber et al., 2017), and marketing (Rahman et al., 2017). Thus, we developed measurement items for evaluating eco-innovation and performance based on a previous study (Zhu, Q. H. et al., 2019). For TEM practices, we developed measurement items, considering the operating situations of SMMEs in China.

三、被动语态使用常见问题（Common problems with writing passive voice）

（1）主语过长的被动句（Top-heavy Passive Sentence）。

在写作中使用被动语态，最常见的问题之一就是主语部分的信息过长，这种句子被称为"top-heavy sentence"。例如：

× Wheat and barley, collected from the Gansu field site, as well as sorghum and millet, collected at Yulin, were adopted.

√ Four cereals were adopted: wheat and barley, collected from the Gansu field site; and sorghum and millet, collected at Yulin.

（2）包含重复信息的被动句（Short repetitive passive sentence），实例见表3-7。

表3-7 包含重复信息的被动句实例

原句 Original Sentence	缺点 Drawbacks	改进后
1. The data were collected and corrections were calculated	be 动词的重复使用	1. The data were collected and corrections calculated
2. The data were collected and they were analyzed using OLS	主语和be 动词的重复使用	2. The data were collected and analyzed using OLS
3. The data which were collected at Site 3 were analyzed using GWR	从句的不必要使用	3. The data collected at Site 3 were analyzed using GWR

★ 请完成以下练习

练习1：试比较下面句子下画线所标出词汇的通用含义与在本句中的学术含义

（1）When cultures reached the late exponential phase, they were divided and put into two sterile flasks.

（2）There is evidence that industrialization has a beneficial effect on distribution by creating jobs (in manufacturing and related sectors) and thus eradicating poverty.

（3）Chiu et al. (2021) used a multiple bounded discrete choice model and found that the elasticity of credit demand is moderately inelastic.

（4）McFadden and Train (2020) showed that a mixed logit model can approximate any logit model.

（5）Through investigating the literature and combining the available indices from a Chinese national commercial bank, the first criteria layer of credit risk assessment is comprised of six feature layers.

词汇	通用含义	学术语境含义
culture	The arts, beliefs, customs, institutions, and other products of human work and thought considered as a particular time or social group（文化）	The growing of microorganisms, tissue cells, or other living matter in a specially prepared nutrient medium（溶液）
distribution	giving or delivering something to a number of people or place（分发）	

(续)

词汇	通用含义	学术语境含义
discrete	(ideas or things) separate and distinct from each other 分离的，不连续的	
approximate	adj. almost correct or accurate 接近的	
layer	a quantity of sth that lies over a surface or between surfaces 层	

练习2：找出下面段落中的合成词，并尝试写出它们的结构及其词根的其他常用形式

(1) Data standardization of evaluation indices. The indices of credit rating can be divided into two categories: the quantitative indices and the qualitative indices. The quantitative indices include interval indices, positive indices and negative indices. This paper uses the Max-Min normalization technique to transform the positive indices and the negative indices.

词汇	含义	结构	其他常用形式
standardization	标准化	standardize+(a)tion	standard, standardize
quantitative			
qualitative			
negative			
normalization			
technique			
transform			

(2) There are strategic sustainability behaviors in SMMEs (small and medium-sized manufacturing enterprises), ranging from resistant, reactive, anticipatory, and innovation-based to sustainability rooted behaviors (Klewitz and Hansen, 2014). SMMEs may adopt eco-innovation at different implementation levels (Daddi et al., 2012) and the underlying reasons include different organizational size and geographical location (Dey et al., 2018), as well as different cultures, supply chain networks, and regulations in the sector (Pacheco et al., 2018).

词汇	含义	结构	其他常用形式
strategic			
anticipatory			
sustainability			
underlying			
geographical			
network			

练习3：用括号中所给的名词替换下画线所标出部分的信息，使下列句子更符合SSCI论文的表达习惯

例如：The number of consumers in the UK market who eat novel foods every year has dramatically increased. (consumption)

The annual consumption of novel food/novel-food consumption in the UK market has dramatically increased.

(1) The Texas High Plains (THP) is a productive agricultural region, and it relies heavily on the exhaustible Ogallala Aquifer for irrigation water for producing crops. (production)

(2) At both locations, treatments were organized as a split-block design and replicated four times. (replication)

(3) Wealth, access to credit from the formal sector and family functioning across regions

in China are substantially heterogenetic. (heterogeneity)

(4) Distributive favoritism can be commonly explained as a form of collective corruption, whereby clients help their patrons steal the money from public coffers. (explanation)

(5) Attributes are product characteristics influencing how consumers choose among different items. (choice)

练习4：将下列句子下画线所标出部分进行名词化变体，使其更加符合SSCI论文写作的表达习惯

例如：A recent report about road safety found people who drive too fast was the primary cause of accidents.

A recent report about road safety found speeding was the primary cause of accidents.

(1) Direct investment was added every year in the first village site for 5 years.

The first village site received ＿＿ of direct investment for 5 years.

(2) Functional analysis of financial stability is also providing insight into how stress is responded and mechanisms regulated in small-medium sized companies.

Functional analysis of financial stability is also providing insight into ＿＿＿＿ in small-medium sized companies.

(3) The rate at which the over-expenditure began to emerge was significantly lower in the consecutively invested villages than in the underinvested villages.

＿＿＿＿＿＿ was significantly lower in the consecutively invested villages than in the underinvested villages.

(4) There are some uncertain situations of projecting research model being assessed by using more than one model or by perturbing model parameters.

＿＿＿＿＿＿ are sometimes assessed by using more than one model or by perturbing model parameters.

(5) According to Formula (2), how coefficient variations of the 19 indices are weighed can be obtained. ...

According to Formula (2), ＿＿＿＿ of the 19 indices can be obtained. ...

第 2 篇

SSCI论文主体写作

第 4 章 引言一：研究背景与文献综述

从整体上观察一篇 SSCI 论文的布局，论文主体的第一个部分一般是"引言"（Introduction，有的期刊叫作"Background"或不加标题）。这个部分的主要功能是为读者理解论文核心内容提供背景信息与研究视角。

"引言"部分从框架结构上来看呈现倒梯形，信息的传递是从一般（起点为介绍该研究所处的宏观研究背景）到具体（落脚处为本研究的研究问题和目的）如图 4-1 所示。

为了更好地理解"引言"部分从一般到具体的倒梯形结构，我们还可以进一步将其细分为六个阶段如图 4-2 所示。

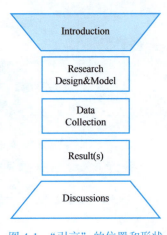

图 4-1 "引言"的位置和形状

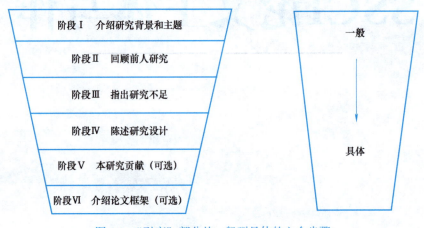

图 4-2 "引言"部分从一般到具体的六个步骤

4.1 引言阶段 I：介绍研究背景和主题

从引言一开始，作者会对相关研究领域进行简要介绍，为读者提供理解研究问题的背景。通过解释广泛研究领域与具体研究问题之间的关系，使读者理解本论文的重要性。

阶段 I 的信息要素包括：

（1）陈述本研究领域的相关重要事实背景

（2）介绍与论文研究主题密切相关的分领域

例 4.1（AE 7）

INTRODUCTION（Stage Ⅰ）

[1]Nowadays, digital financial services represent one of the main Big Data sources. [2]In fact, in the last two years, the global payments' revenue has grown of 12%, reaching the value of 1.9 trillion dollars in 2018 (McKinsey, 2010) by processing 14 trillion financial transactions per day. [3]The wide use of financial services has focused the attention of researchers on the credit risk management for developing models aiming, on one hand, to reduce financial risks and, on the other hand, to increase the related profits. [4]According to Basel Committee on Banking Supervision (BCBS), banking risks can be classified in: (ⅰ) credit, (ⅱ) market and (ⅲ) operational risks. [5]As described in Buehler et al. (2008), about 60% of the banks' threat is represented by credit risks, mainly due to the emerging of Social Lending Platform, also known as Peer-to-Peer (P2P) lending.

标题为"A benchmark of machine learning approaches for credit score prediction"的这篇文章的宏观背景：在过去数十年的金融市场，由于社会贷款平台（social lending platform）的不断涌现，传统的信贷风险评估与管理系统无法有效预测其风险，因此增加了信贷市场的风险。基于此，文章提出一种基于常见信用风险评分模型的基准模型，用以预测P2P平台（即社会平台）贷款的违约风险。本文引言阶段Ⅰ的框架分析如图4-3所示。

图 4-3　引言阶段Ⅰ的例文框架分析（一）

可以看出，论文作者利用"引言"的第一部分，将研究的宏观背景（句1），研究的分领域（句3）及具体的研究对象（句5）进行了介绍。这个介绍过程，是一个逐步缩小范围和聚焦的过程。

例 4.2（AE 8）

INTRODUCTION（Stage Ⅰ）

[1]Given the reformation of agricultural credit policies in China in the 21st century, it is important to understand the drivers of credit demand and any informational and/or institutional gaps between lenders and borrowers (Kong et al., 2014; Turvey et al., 2014; Cao et al., 2016). [2]By and large, the literature related to agricultural finance in China mostly investigates the characteristics of the borrower with surprisingly few examining agricultural credit as a consumer product characterized by a bundle of attributes of varying importance to farmer-borrowers.

本文"Heterogeneous choice in the demand for agriculture credit in China: results from an in-the-field choice experiment"为了考察农户信贷的属性偏好和支付意愿，首先调查了中国农村农户的信贷需求状况。本文引言阶段Ⅰ的框架分析如图4-4所示。

| 句1: Given the reformation of agricultural credit policies in China in the 21st century, it is important to understand **the drivers of credit demand** | 鉴于中国21世纪的农业信贷政策，理解信贷需求的动因就显得非常重要 | 研究背景 |

| 句2: The literature related to agricultural finance in China mostly investigates the characteristics of the borrower with surprisingly few examining **agricultural credit as a consumer product** characterized by a bundle of attributes of varying importance to farmer-borrowers | 在中国，大多数农村金融文献调查借款人的特点，很少将涉农信贷作为一种消费品去分析。这类研究挖掘涉农借款人具有的不同特征属性以及这些特征属性对信用风险影响的重要性次序 | 研究领域 |

图4-4 引言阶段Ⅰ的例文框架分析（二）

引言阶段Ⅰ的主要目的是陈述相关研究背景和研究事实，在动词时态的选择上多采用**现在时态（present tense）**来强调事实被广泛接受的程度。

4.2 引言阶段Ⅱ：引述前人相关研究

在引言的第二阶段，作者使用相关文献来证明他们研究的合理性，并进一步引导读者了解该研究问题的研究现状。通过评述他人的研究，作者才能表明在本领域尚未完成和需要完成的工作的重要性，为提出现有研究的价值和意义打下基础。

值得注意的是，文献综述（Literature Review 或 Related Work）在相当一部分SSCI论文中的位置是以单独的一个部分出现在引言（Introduction）之后的。但不管位置如何，其基本功能是一致的。

4.2.1 文献引述的组织形式

常见的文献引述组织形式有以下两种类型：

（1）按照文献的主题与本研究主题的相关性排列，如图4-5所示。

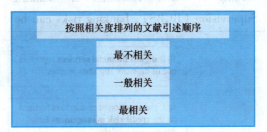

图4-5 按照主题相关性进行文献引述

例4.3（AE 13）

INTRODUCTION（Stage Ⅱ）

¹The literature has extensively investigated the socioeconomic, institutional, and cultural factors underpinning the demand for sons. Studies point to the relatively low adult female earnings in traditional agrarian economies as constituting an important factor in the persistence of son preference（Ben-Porath and Welch 1976, Rosenzweig and Schultz 1982, Ahn 1995, Qian 2008）. Das Gupta et al.（2013）suggest that adult sons' support of elderly parents also contributes to the persistence of son preference in China, India,

and South Korea. Edlund (1999) relates son preference to institutional factors such as the caste system in India. Alesina et al. (2013) explore historical origins of crosscultural differences in the role of women in society and find that traditional agricultural practices, such as plowing, influenced the historical gender division of labor as well as the evolution of gender norms.

²Incorporating insights from behavioral economics, our paper is the first attempt in the literature to propose and test an insurance motive underpinning son preference. This approach is closely related to a broader literature linking economic preferences to economic outcomes (see, e.g., Dohmen et al. 2011, Sutter et al. 2013, Noussair et al. 2014, Dimmock et al. 2015). More specifically, compared to daughters, sons have higher agricultural productivity and are expected to shoulder more of the additional responsibility of caring for their parents. Hence, sons are perceived as a better source of insurance for old age in traditional societies in which environmental and social risks are pervasive.

上文在引言阶段Ⅱ回顾了性别偏好背景下对男孩偏好存在的原因。在第一段，作者综述了从政治经济学、社会制度及文化三个维度产生的男孩偏好的原因。在第二段，基于行为经济学视角，作者进一步综述了从经济偏好（economic preferences）角度出发产生性别偏好的原因。体现了与要研究主题相关性的逐层递进。

使用此种方式进行的文献引述，最先引用的文献与在下一阶段［第三阶段］提出的研究问题相关度最低，但这并不意味着作者引述的文献与本研究主题毫不相干。一般这些文献与更接近主题的文献之间遵循时间上的发展顺序或存在必要的逻辑关联。

（2）按照文献的不同类别进行排列，如图4-6所示。

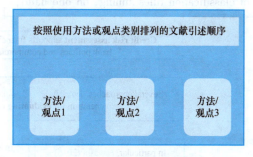

图4-6 按照类别进行文献引述

例4.4（AE 7）

¹Credit risk assessment supports financial institutes in defining bank policies and commercial strategies. According to Wu et al. (2014) financial risk assessment is characterized by the following three properties: interconnection, dependence, and complexity. After the 2008 financial crisis, credit risk scoring has increasingly grown in importance becoming a critical means in credit risk management. In particular, it aims to support practitioners in the decision making process about loan's assignment to an applicant on the basis of different parameters.

²Several approaches (Hayashi, 2016; Soui et al., 2019) rely on rules generation for evaluating credit risks. In particular, Hayashi (2016) generated a set of rules by three versions of Re-RX algorithm to evaluate credit risk from a Pareto optimal perspective. However, this approach is difficult to apply on large amounts of data due to different issues in the rules generation process.

³In a similar way, in Soui et al. (2019) a credit risk evaluation model based on multi optimization strategy produced a set of classification rules aiming, on one hand, to minimize the complexity of the generated solution, and, on the other hand, to maximize weights representing rules importance.

上文文献引用框架分析如图4-7所示。

```
┌─────────────────────────────────────────┐      ┌──────────┐
│ Credit risk assessment supports         │      │信贷风险评估│
│ financial institutes in defining        │      │的重要性   │
│ bank policies and commercial strategies.│      └──────────┘
└─────────────────────────────────────────┘
                    ↓
┌─────────────────────────────────────────┐      ┌──────────┐
│ Several approaches (Hayashi, 2016;      │      │已有研究通过│
│ Soui et al., 2019) rely on rules        │      │规则生成来评│
│ generation for evaluating credit risks. │      │估信贷风险 │
└─────────────────────────────────────────┘      └──────────┘
                    ↓
┌──────────────────────┐ ┌──────────────────┐    ┌──────────┐
│In particular, Hayashi│ │In a similar way, │    │分别回顾评估│
│(2016) generated a set│ │in Soui et al.    │    │的两种方法 │
│of rules by three     │ │(2019) a credit   │    └──────────┘
│versions of Re-RX     │ │risk evaluation   │
│algorithm to evaluate │ │model based on    │
│credit risk from a    │ │multi-optimization│
│Pareto optimal        │ │strategy produced │
│perspective.          │ │a set of          │
│                      │ │classification    │
│                      │ │rules importance  │
└──────────────────────┘ └──────────────────┘
```

图4-7 引言阶段Ⅱ的例文框架分析

例4.5（AE 9）

INTRODUCTION（Stage Ⅱ）

¹Despite nearly two decades of development of LF* in China, previous studies have paid scant attention to its temporal fluctuation and the significant effects of important events at certain points in time (Wang, 2016). ²Certain progress has been made with regard to the spatial difference. ³Qualitative induction (Niu and Wu, 2012), descriptive statistics (Wang, 2011), and clustering methods (Wang and Tang, 2013) were used to analyse the regional differences in LF.

*LF: Land Finance 土地金融

上文在文献综述部分回顾了中国土地金融的时空变化（spatio-temporal changes of land finance）。具体分为定性归纳（qualitative induction）、描述性统计（descriptive statistics）和聚类分析（clustering）。这三种方法以并列方式进行陈述，也是文献综述最常见的组织形式之一。

4.2.2　文内引用的语言策略

所谓"**文内引用**（in-text citation）"，是在正文中对来自作者原创事实和观点以外资源的简短引用。它通常包括文献的作者和发表时间，或指向能在参考文献中找到的该资源具体发表信息的编号。具体的两种引用格式见表4-1。

表4-1　APA[⊖]格式下的引用

"数字编号"型引用	"人名+年份"型引用
The Chinese central government, in publicly available documents from 2004 to 2015, has reinforced the importance of agriculture, with the countryside and farmers receiving much of the spotlight in terms of criticality to China's development [24]	Rural tourism in China is a relatively recent phenomenon, if we compare China with the situation in Organization for Co-operation and Development (OECD) countries, where such development increased markedly after the 1970s, generating local social and economic multipliers (Perales, 2002)

⊖ APA格式是由美国心理学会（the American Psychological Association）制定的，在社会科学学术论文写作中广泛使用的一种格式。http：//www.apastyle.org/.

除了了解基本的引用格式之外，还应该了解作者在引用时想要强调的信息及强调的形式。基于不同的引用意图，文内引用的引用强调形式可分为三类：

（1）作者显著型引用（Author Prominent Citation）

例 4.6（AE 10）

> INTRODUCTION（Stage Ⅱ）
>
> [1]The effect of human activity in the process of vegetation restoration is debatable. [2]For example, Li et al. (2011) considered that climate change was a decisive factor affecting the growth of vegetation, and in the meantime, human activities could accelerate the rate of vegetation change in the short term; Zhao et al. (2016) found that human activities had double effects on vegetation changes, and their constructive role was stronger than their destructive effect; Alix-Garcia et al. (2016) provided a case study showing that political and economic transition could bring huge changes in vegetation coverage; Qu et al. (2018) concluded that ecological restoration projects were the main factor for vegetation restoration, while the benefits were closely related to the combined effect of the topography, climate, and human management.

如例 4.6 所示，作者显著型引用在引用时将作者姓名及发表年份放在引用信息之前，使用不同的报告动词（reporting verbs）和不同的时态（verb tenses），提示本论文作者（后简称"论文作者"）对所引用的研究作者（后简称"研究作者"）的观点和事实的接受程度见表 4-2。

表 4-2 "作者显著型引用"的功能及时态

作 者	报告动词	从句引导词 that	引用内容	引用的功能及时态
Pingali and Khwaja (2004)	argue	that	globalization, along with economic growth, **has triggered** Indian household adoption of a food culture that **is** different from the traditional patterns	广泛接受的事实或发现（一般现在时）
Lu and Qi (2013)	claimed	that	there **were** differences between the environmental health effects in countries or areas	某一特定研究的发现或事实（一般过去时）
Nouna et al. (2003)	suggested	that	that the dates of silking and grain-filling **must be** precisely predicted so as to increase the simulation accuracy of leaf expansion and senescence	观点或建议而非发现或事实（情态动词）
According to Namvar et al. (2018)			credit scoring predictive models **can be** classified into two categories: statistical approaches and artificial intelligence methods	

在使用作者显著型引用时，论文作者对所引用的事实和观点的态度会影响到动词时态的选择。根据其确定程度的差异，在陈述信息部分动词的时态可以选择现在时态、过去时态或情态动词。

1）当引用的信息为普遍接受的科学事实时，动词使用一般现在时态；

2）当引用的信息是已发表的具体研究结果时，采用一般过去时态；

3）当研究作者观点被认为确定程度不

高，或引用信息为建议而非科学发现和观点时，论文作者会使用确定程度低的报告动词或情态动词。

（2）作者弱显著型引用（Weak-author Prominent Citation）

作者弱显著型引用与作者显著型引用的格式相同，都是将作者姓名及发表年份放在引用信息的前面。不同之处在于，作者弱显著型引用不强调作者观点和态度，只说明事实。

例 4.7（AE 9）

INTRODUCTION（Stage Ⅱ）
[1]In view of these risks, China's LF* sustainability problem has attracted wide attention from scholars. Liu（2014）qualitatively and comprehensively reviewed the problem of unsustainable LF; Geng et al.（2018）empirically tested the LF sustainability at national scale; while a majority of studies analysed separate effects of LF in terms of farmland loss, environmental problems, and social warfare（Zheng et al., 2014; Zhang and Xu, 2017）. Internationally, El-Nagdy et al.（2018）credibly pointed out the potential socio-economic risks from using public-owned lands as mortgage for urban infrastructure financing applying a qualitative comparative analysis approach, and Valtonen et al.（2017）expounded the LF risk management strategies of Finland and the Netherlands in the process of public land development adopting case studies.
*LF: Land Finance 土地金融

例 4.7 中使用的动词（短语）如 review、test、point out、expound 都用于描述研究者的行为，其语言功能在于引出该研究者的观点或成果，不强调论文作者本人的立场。

（3）信息显著型引用（Information-prominent Citation）

信息显著型引用是将引用信息放在作者姓名及发表年份的前面，以突出信息本身的文内引用形式。

例 4.8（AE 11）

INTRODUCTION（Stage Ⅱ）
The climate impacts in different regions are likely to show large differences（3, 4）, with some countries suffering disproportionately serious consequences without the adaptation of early and stringent climate change mitigation policies（5, 6）. For some less-developed states that are endowed with rich natural resources, half of their existing species may be in danger of extinction（7）, and many coastal regions may be exposed to multiple risks of diseases resulting from climate change（8）. Even worse, the imbalanced distribution of loss and damage will exacerbate the inequal trends of economic development across countries（9）.

例 4.9（AE 12）

INTRODUCTION（Stage Ⅱ）
Manufacturing industries in developed countries appeared to be substituting toward high-skill workers despite rising skill prices, suggesting that these industries were experiencing a skill-biased demand shift that emanated logically from the adoption of new technology（Berman et al. 1998）. Although trade in the form of offshoring may produce such demand shifts, its modest scale in the 1980s and early 1990s meant that its estimated impacts were far smaller than those

of investments in high-tech capital and equipment (Feenstra & Hanson 1999). Finally, simple factor-content calibration exercises—which rescaled traded-good imports into embodied labor imports—found that rising trade integration could account for only a small part of the fall in relative wages of low-skill workers in the United States (Borjas et al. 1997, Krugman 2000). When Richard Freeman asked in 1995 if US wages were "being set in Beijing," his answer was an emphatic no (Freeman 1995).

信息显著型引用将信息作为引用重点。我们看到例4.8和例4.9的引述部分在动词时态的选择上同样具有多样性。作者对于动词的选择可以参照之前介绍"作者显著型引用"时提到的动词选用标准见表4-2。

课外拓展与练习

★ 请完成以下练习

练习1：下列段落分别为论文 "Introduction" 部分的阶段 I 信息。请将下列句子重新排序，使其更符合信息表达的特征

例：

[1]To some extent, people can control the environmental factors that make it difficult to focus. [2] Many things interrupt people's ability to focus on a task: distractions, headaches, noises. [3] Can people increase their ability to focus simply by eating regularly? [4]However, what about internal factors, such as empty stomach?

正确顺序：2—1—4—3

(1)

[1]The government has implemented, most recently via the 2020 National Food Security Act (NFSA), an extensive set of public policy measures to ensure that sufficient food is available to the poorest and most vulnerable in society. [2]However, while these policies have been in place, there has been a decline in cereal consumption in Sri Lanka. [3]Improving food security and nutrition intake remains a key policy concern in developing countries and Sri Lanka is no exception.[4] In addition, there is also the Integrated Child Development Scheme (ICDS) that help ensure access to food at the household level.

正确顺序：_____

(2)

[1]The volume of migration within the region is increasing substantially and the intra-ASEAN migrants have more than quadrupled, from 2.1 million in 1995 to 9.9 million in 2016. [2]Southeast Asia (SEA) is an important player in global migration constituting a significant portion of the total international migrants. [3]International mobilities have become one of the most significant realities in this modern world. [4] Skille migration is emerging as the new wave when the migrants begin to flow between countries both in the Global North and in the Global South.

正确顺序：____ ____ ____

(3)

[1]Clinical trials are under way to assess the efficacy of a variety of antiviral drugs. [2] Coronavirus Disease 2019 (COVID-19) caused 2 million cases and more than 150,000 deaths worldwide as of mid-April 2020. [3]

However, many of these drugs have toxicities and thus far no drug has been proven to improve outcomes in patients with COVID-19.

正确顺序：_____ _____ _____

练习2：将下列"引用"部分的例句与其对应功能配对

引 用	功 能
1. A suspect case of the COVID-19 refers to a person with clinical signs and symptoms suggestive of pneumonia (Zhou 2020)	a. 举例子 b. 指出研究不足 c. 下定义 d. 介绍研究背景 e. 讨论研究方法可行性 f. 回顾研究方法
2. With the continuous development of the rural economy and the deepening of the rural financial reform process, the characteristics of rural credit demand continues to be of economic importance and significance to agricultural growth (Nan et al., 2019; Tian et al., 2020)	
3. Understanding the demand side of rural credit is crucial. For example, recent policy initiatives to increase credit supply will be more effective if aggregate credit demand was highly elastic and less so if inelastic (Ma and Xu, 2018)	
4. Turvey et al. (2012) used a multiple bounded discrete choice model and found that the elasticity of credit demand is moderately inelastic (about 0.61 on average) with about 25% of farmers having demand elasticities less than 1.0	
5. While a recent systematic review shows that women's SHGs have positive effects on economic and political empowerment (Brody et al., 2017), there is limited evidence on their effect on women's empowerment in agriculture and no evidence on how they affect men within these households	
6. Starting with an estimation of a Cobb-Douglas production function, we find that for the average manufacturing firm in the formal sector the output elasticity of public capital is about 0.16, in line with the broad range of empirical evidence reported in the meta-analysis by Bom and Ligthart (2014)	

1—___ 2—___ 3—___ 4—___ 5—___ 6—___

第5章 引言二：陈述现有研究

在上一章，我们了解了作者如何在引言阶段Ⅰ和阶段Ⅱ介绍研究背景和进行文献引述。本章将介绍SSCI论文作者如何利用引言的后半部分陈述本研究取得的创新。这个部分包含阶段Ⅲ至阶段Ⅵ四个部分如图5-1所示。

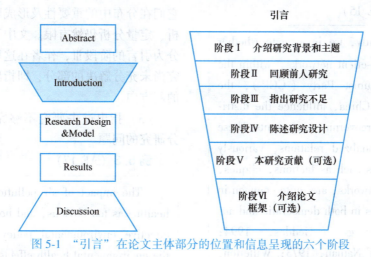

图5-1 "引言"在论文主体部分的位置和信息呈现的六个阶段

5.1 引言阶段Ⅲ：指出研究不足

在这个阶段，作者往往使用一个简短的句子来指出在前人研究基础上，本研究领域存在的研究缺口或不足（Research Gap），为表明本研究的重要性和价值做好铺垫。

5.1.1 引言阶段Ⅲ的信息要素

研究缺口或不足，是指本研究的研究现状存在的问题或与期望值之间存在的差距。SSCI论文需要作者在引言部分清晰呈现本研究的研究缺口。

根据此阶段的语言功能，信息要素一般涉及以下三个功能中的一个。

（1）指出过去研究在理论或方法上存在的漏洞、差异或分歧。

例5.1（AE 16）

Countries and banks typically use varying credit evaluation systems*; the variety of these credit evaluation systems is still expanding. Banks need to invest significant labor and resources for collecting these large volumes and high varieties of data. Determining data attributes that are useful or useless (redundant), is still a concern. Credit evaluation is complex making it difficult to effectively assess borrower creditworthiness. However, significant aspects of this complexity are omitted in standard discriminatory and predictive approaches such as multiple regression techniques*.

* credit evaluation systems 信用评估体系　multiple regression techniques 多元回归方法

本段引言介绍"信用评价复杂性（complexity of credit evaluation）"的重要意义，指出现有的如"多元回归方法"等标准的判别和预测方法忽略了研究信用评价复杂性的重要方面，例5.1下画线标出部分指出了现有研究方法存在的不足。

（2）基于现有研究对同一研究问题进一步探索的新方向。

例5.2（AE 15）

> In this study, we investigate whether and how patron-client networks* within the Chinese Communist Party (CCP), the ruling party of China, influence the distribution of intergovernmental grants. These informal, personalized relations, variously called by names such as factions, cliques, or patronage networks, are quite common in dominant parties in both democratic and authoritarian settings (Geddes, 1994; Grindle, 1977; Nathan, 1973; Willerton, 1992). Most of the existing studies have focused on these networks' role in facilitating elite advancement* (e.g., Jia et al., 2015; Shih et al., 2012). Some qualitative and ethnographic studies* suggest that such networks might also serve as an important mechanism for allocating resources (Bettcher, 2005; Hillman, 2014; Ike, 1972), but systematic, quantitative analysis on how and why they matter in distribution remains limited.
>
> * patron-client networks 赞助人-客户网络　elite advancement 精英晋升　qualitative and ethnographic studies 定性与民族志研究

本段引言首先介绍本文的研究目标——"'中国共产党党内的赞助人-客户网络关系（patron-client networks within the Chinese Communist Party）'是否及如何影响'政府间拨款的分配（the distribution of intergovernmental grants）'"。在进行文献回顾时，作者指出现有研究多聚焦于"这种网络关系在促进精英晋升方面的作用（these networks' role in facilitating elite advancement）及作为分配资源的机制作用（an important mechanism for allocating resources）"，但对它们在分布中的重要性及形成原因的系统分析、定量分析仍然有限。文中下画线标出部分为引言的阶段Ⅲ，作者在这里指出原有研究尚未充分解决的部分，即指出了研究发展的新方向。

（3）指出过去研究不够完善或尚未充分研究的问题。

例5.3（AE 17）

> The impact of air pollution on public health was too obvious, and how to develop effective environmental policy to improve the environmental health effects had become the focus of researchers. Wong et al. (1998) found that SO_2 emissions decreased by approximately 80% after the implementation of the policy when studying environmental policies for sulphur fuels in Hong Kong. Brooks and Sethi (1997) noted in their study that the people who are most exposed to air pollutants, including tenants, have low incomes and poor education. Ebenstein (2012) showed that the risks of cancer and other diseases of families with tap water or clean water resources were significantly lower than for other families. Lu and Qi (2013) claimed that there were differences between the environmental health effects in countries or areas, and environmental health risk depended on different levels of education, environment and health

> and other public services. Although those studies analyzed the impacts of air pollution on public health from several perspectives, there have been few studies on the spatial spillover* of air pollution and the spatial effect on public health.
>
> *spatial spillover 空间溢出效应

本段引言首先陈述"改善环境健康效应的环境政策（develop effective environmental policy to improve the environmental health effects）"已成为研究焦点。在对此研究方向进行综述基础上，作者在本段末尾指出"但空气污染的'空间溢出效应（spatial spillover）'和'对公众健康的空间影响

例 5.4（AE 19）

（the spatial effect on public health）'的研究却很少"。文中下画线标出部分为引言的阶段Ⅲ，作者在这部分评论过去研究不够完善的地方并提出值得进一步扩展的新问题。

5.1.2 研究现状与研究不足的交替进行

需要注意的是，不是所有论文中，引言部分信息排列的顺序都是按照从阶段Ⅰ到阶段Ⅵ依次出现。在有些论文中，会看到阶段Ⅰ（介绍研究背景和主题）、阶段Ⅱ（回顾前人研究）与阶段Ⅲ（指出研究不足）多次交替出现，为本文研究目的的介绍和研究贡献的陈述做好铺垫。例子见表 5-1。

表 5-1 引言部分阶段Ⅰ至阶段Ⅲ反复出现示例

论 文 内 容	阶　　段
Firms face multiple growth constraints in developing countries, including the lack of access to markets, decrepit energy, and transportation infrastructure, and lack of security	阶段Ⅰ 介绍研究背景和主题 发展中国家企业面临诸多发展限制
[1]A large and still growing literature, however, has documented the importance of financing constraints for small firms, especially in less developed countries (Ayyagari, Demirguc-Kunt, & Maksimovic, 2008; Beck, Demirguc-Kunt, & Maksimovic, 2005). [2]A recent controversy has focused on the relative importance of formal versus informal financial providers for alleviating firms' financing constraints in developing countries	阶段Ⅱ 回顾前人研究 在发展中国家，降低小型企业融资限制的正规与非正规融资渠道的相对重要性引起学界广泛关注
Even less is known, however, about micro- or household-based enterprises, especially in rural China	阶段Ⅲ 指出研究不足 但是，对于中国农村地区微型企业及家庭企业，此方面的研究不足
Given the lack of formal financial statements, microenterprises face severe information asymmetries in developing countries, which hinder the credit availability from formal financial institutions, such as banks and credit cooperatives	阶段Ⅰ 介绍研究背景和主题 发展中国家微型企业面临的信息不对称阻碍了其从银行和信用合作社等正规金融机构获得贷款
[1]Informal finance may therefore be essential for microenterprises in China under its special economic and legal institutions (Allen et al., 2005) and especially in rural areas that have experienced a withdrawal of formal financial institutions since the mid-1990s. [2]On the other hand, formal finance might be more effective in alleviating financing constraints, as informal finance carries high interest rates, is of limited scale, and has pro-cyclical trends	阶段Ⅱ 回顾前人研究 在中国特殊的经济和法律制度下，正规渠道融资和非正规渠道融资对微型企业的重要性回顾
It is therefore a priori not clear whether micro- and household-based enterprises can benefit more from informal or formal financing sources in rural China, which leaves the question for empirical research	阶段Ⅲ 指出研究不足 中国农村微型企业和家庭企业究竟从非正规融资渠道获益更多，还是从正式融资渠道获益更多，这一问题尚待实证研究

5.1.3 引言阶段Ⅲ的语言特征

阶段Ⅲ的语言信号非常明显，作者常用含有"no""few/little""remain a mystery"或"not studied/examined"等词来说明目前研究的不足之处。这个部分的句子基本结构总结见表5-2和表5-3。

表5-2 指出研究不足的基本句型一

信号词	研究不足	研究话题
However But	few studies have reported on	
	there is little information available on	the dynamic of altitudinal change
	even less is known about	

表5-3 指出研究不足的基本句型二

连接词	研究现状	研究不足
Although While	some literature is available on X	
	many studies have been done on X	little information is available on Y
	much research has been devoted to X	

除以上基本句型外，也会存在一些变体，但读者很容易通过这些语言信号如连词"But, However"；限定词"little, few"；形容词"limited, scarce, under researched"；动词"ignore"等捕捉到这个阶段作者想要表达的研究不足之处。我们来看2012年发表在《金融学学报》上的一篇关于信贷风险的研究论文引言：

例 5.5 （AE 20）

It is widely recognized that the credit spread* reflects not only a default premium* determined by the firm's credit risk but also a liquidity premium* due to illiquidity of the secondary debt market (e.g., Longstaff, Mithal, and Neis (2005) and Chen, Lesmond, and Wei (2007)). *However*, academics and policy makers tend to treat both the default premium and the liquidity premium as independent, and thus *ignore* interactions between them. The financial crisis of 2007 to 2008 demonstrates the importance of such an interaction-deterioration in debt market liquidity caused severe financing difficulties for many financial firms, which in turn exacerbated their credit risk.

* credit spread 信用利差 default premium 违约风险溢价 liquidity premium 流动性风险溢价

5.2 引言阶段Ⅳ：陈述研究设计（目的）

在此阶段，一篇SSCI论文的引言信息已经正式聚焦在了本研究。作者一般会直接简明地阐述本文的研究活动如何设计与开展，或（并）介绍本研究的研究目的，以说明本研究如何解决阶段Ⅲ中指出的研究缺陷或不足。

5.2.1 引言阶段Ⅳ的语言特征

在介绍本研究时，阶段Ⅳ的句法形式以论文导向型表达（俞炳丰[10]）为主要特征。**论文导向型表达**的主要目的为介绍研究本身的内容，作者会直接使用如"purpose""aim"或"paper"等信号词来陈述研究的设计及思路，或（和）使用"we analyze/summarize"等引导的宾语从句来描述研究的设计、思路及主要发现。示例见表5-4。

第 5 章　引言二：陈述现有研究

表 5-4　示例

例子	文章	论文导向型描述句型 1	论文导向型描述句型 2
例 5.6	AE 4	This paper estimates and analyzes the effect of external capital from China, including foreign aid and overseas direct investment (ODI), on economic growth in African countries	We find that China's aid has significant positive effects on African economic growth
例 5.7	AE 1	The overall goal of this study is to assess the implications of COVID-19 and related disease control measures for China's rural population and economy	To do so, we have three specific objectives. First, we seek to identify…. Second, we describe the efforts that …. Finally, we present the implications of disease control measures…
例 5.8	AE 18	This paper exploits a field experiment to assess the extent to which lack of information about urban employee health insurance and pension programs contributes to low participation among rural migrants	From the estimated change in demand, we calculate the welfare gain from the information intervention

5.2.2　研究设计（目的）与文献综述的交替进行

在有一些 SSCI 论文中，我们还会看到作者基于研究目的展开文献评述。

例 5.9（AE 14）

论文内容	阶　段
One key determinant that we examine in this paper, which has been under-researched within the existing literature, is the changing pattern of consumer preferences	阶段Ⅳ　陈述研究设计 消费偏好的变化模式
Past studies on nutrition transition indicate that food preferences have been significantly influenced by the progress of economic development (Popkin, 1999; Thow, 2009; Kearney, 2010). In particular, urbanization and trade liberalization increase the variety and availability of food products and thus enable households to diversify their diets, and alter their preferences	阶段Ⅱ　回顾前人研究 对影响饮食偏好的经济因素进行综述
Existing studies account for changes in food preferences by adding time trends (Banks et al., 1997; Mittal, 2007), extrapolating data given parameter estimates (Dong and Fuller, 2010) or correlating time-varying demographic characteristics which are used as proxy variables for consumer preferences with consumption (Moro et al., 2000)	阶段Ⅱ　回顾前人研究 进一步评述量化饮食偏好变化的方法
So we follow an alternative empirical strategy proposed by Chavas (1983) who observed that changing consumer preferences will be exhibited as changing demand elasticities over time	阶段Ⅳ　陈述研究设计 以需求弹性变化测量消费偏好变化

5.3 引言阶段Ⅴ：表明研究贡献（可选）

钱颖一[11]指出，现代经济学作为一种研究经济现象或行为的分析方法或框架，需要具备三个基本要素：视点（Perspective）、参照（Benchmark）、分析方法（Analytical Tools）。在陈述研究贡献或价值时，作者一般会参照这三个要素，从视角的创新、对象的创新及方法的创新介绍本文的研究贡献或创新点。

5.3.1 陈述创新的研究视角、对象或方法

例5.10（AE 5）

> INTRODUCTION（Stage Ⅴ）
>
> There are two novel components to our empirical design. First, India offers the perfect landscape to examine these issues. By focusing on a specific country, using data from a consistent data source and exploiting predetermined cross-state variation in socio economic conditions, we alleviate problems associated with cross-country studies. Second, we incorporate the policy changes in our empirical design to address endogeneity concerns.

本段引言指出现有研究在视角和方法上的创新。首先是从印度这个具体国家出发保证数据来源的一致性（a consistent data source）；其次，是将政策变化（policy changes）纳入实证设计，以解决内生性问题（endogeneity concerns）。

例5.11（AE 10）

> INTRODUCTION（Stage Ⅴ）
>
> In order to overcome the shortcomings of classical statistics models in current vegetation restoration evaluation, this study introduced GWR* to provide a decision-making basis for better implementation of vegetation restoration planning in the future.
>
> *GWR: Geographically weighted regression model 地理加权回归模型

为了克服传统统计模型在植被恢复（vegetation restoration）评估中的缺点，本段引言指出本研究方法上的创新——引入了地理加权回归模型（GWR）为今后更好地实施植被恢复规划提供决策依据。

5.3.2 陈述对现有文献的拓展

例5.12（AE 14）

> INTRODUCTION（Stage Ⅴ）
>
> In this paper, we add to the literature investigating the nutrition transition in two significant ways. First, we capture changes in food preferences in the rural and urban context by estimating time varying household level price and expenditure (income) elasticities 1987-2012. Second, not only do we generate standard elasticity estimates but we also estimate 'preference-based' elasticities.

本段引言明确指出我们对于现有文献的贡献在于从两个重要方面开展"营养迁移（nutrition transition）"的研究。

例5.13（AE 23）

> The contribution of our paper can be better evaluated by relating it to two closely related studies, namely Datta (2012) and Ghani et al. (2015), who also examine the spatial effects of India's Golden Quadrilateral project on plant-level production and find positive benefits for formal sector firms. We extend and refine their findings in several important directions.

第 5 章　引言二：陈述现有研究

本段引言明确指出本研究对于现有文献的贡献在于对 Datta（2012）和 Ghani et al. (2015) 两篇文献研究成果的扩展及改进。

5.3.3　陈述对本领域研究的边际贡献

例 5.14（AE 16）

> The contribution of this paper includes the development of a new integrative methodology that combines the fuzzy rough set theory and fuzzy C-means. Another contribution is developing insights and relevance of complex relationships between farmer characteristics, contextual environmental factors and creditworthiness in China. More broadly, this study provides initial evidence and relationships for generalized evaluation rules for financial institutions to predict creditworthiness of farmers. This study also addresses some of the methodological issues facing previous techniques applied to credit evaluation, especially correlative econometric models.

本段引言从创新的研究方法（a new integrative methodology, some of the methodological issues facing previous techniques）和研究视角（insights and relevance of complex relationships）指出本研究对于现有文献的边际贡献。

论文中常采用以下句型来描述本研究的研究贡献，见表5-5。

表 5-5　表明研究贡献的基本句型

Our paper	contribute (s) to	the recent debate	on	the enhancing policies of rural financial market in China
This paper	adds to	the literature		the persistence of human capital spillovers (Waldinger 2010)
We	contribute (s) to			the slack literature in two ways
Our study				three strands of literature

5.4　引言阶段Ⅵ：介绍论文框架（可选）

SSCI 论文也可以在引言结尾处介绍本文的结构框架。一篇论文中是否包含这个可选项主要取决于学科和 SSCI 期刊的具体要求。因此在阅读 SSCI 论文时读者们可以特别留意这一点。

例 5.15（AE 23）

> INTRODUCTION (Stage Ⅵ)
>
> The rest of the paper is organized as follows. Section 2 presents the main mechanisms of the empirical analysis using a stylized model, Section 3 discusses the data and summary statistics, while Section 4 describes the empirical specification and the identification strategy. Section 5 reports the results of the empirical analysis, and Section 6 concludes.

例 5.16（AE 14）

> INTRODUCTION (Stage Ⅵ)
>
> This paper is structured as follows. In section 2 we describe our data as well as the adjustment of unit values. Section 3 details our estimation methodology. Section 4 presents the various demand elasticity estimates. In section 5, we perform two simulation exercises to understand how these changes in elasticities affect food consumption behavior. We highlight the limitations in section 6 and conclude in section 7.

在介绍论文框架时，要注意动词选择的多样性。此阶段的常用句型可以总结为以下三类：

（1）句型1，见表5-6。

表5-6 句型1示例

		introduce
In Section I	we	discuss
		describe
		perform
		highlight
		conclude

（2）句型2，见表5-7。

表5-7 句型2示例

	reviews
	reports
In Section II	discusses
	details
	highlights
	concludes

（3）句型3，见表5-8。

表5-8 句型3示例

A brief literature review	is contained	in Section 2
Data and summary statistics	are introduced	in Section 3

课外拓展与练习

★请完成以下练习

练习1：将下列句型与对应的语言功能配对。

1. 介绍研究背景
2. 介绍研究目的
3. 描述研究方法
4. 指出研究不足

（1）功能：_____
- In this paper, we address this discrepancy/we present our model...
- The purpose/aim/objective of this investigation/study was to determine/analyze/evaluate...

（2）功能：_____
- It has been increasingly recognized as serious, worldwide public health concern...
- Over the past decade, one of the most important advances in... has been the development of...

（3）功能：_____
- There has not yet been a consistent approach among different studies/laboratories.
- There are relatively few studies evaluating the risk associated with the forms.

（4）功能：_____
- In this study, we studied the first transcriptome of... samples from three developmental stages...
- We conducted an analysis of... without treatment and following... extraction in order to explore extraction effects on...

练习2：用正确的动词形式填空

（A）As part of the Paris Agreement, nearly all countries ___(1)___ (agree) to take steps to limit the global surface average temperature increase to less than 2℃ or 1.5℃ compared with preindustrial levels. Although both the 2℃ and 1.5℃ goals have been discussed frequently since the Copenhagen Accord in 2009, most research efforts ___(2)___ (focus) on the 2℃ target. The 1.5℃ goal ___(3)___ (begin) to receive considerable attention only after it was formally adopted in the Paris Agreement, and a minority of studies since, particularly at the country level, have been conducted ___(4)___ (use) it. Still, research has now shown that there ___(5)___ (be) important differences between a 2℃ and

1.5℃ warming; for example, the economic cost to reach the 1.5℃ goal ___(6)___ (be) at least threefold that of the 2℃ goal. The Intergovernmental Panel on Climate Change (IPCC) ___(7)___ (release) a special report in 2019 on the impacts of global warming of 1.5℃ above preindustrial levels and the related greenhouse gas emission pathways. Nevertheless, current studies on the 1.5℃ goal are far from adequate to be enough for the sixth assessment report (AR 6) on climate change that is due to ___(8)___ (release) in 2022.

(B) China's one-quarter century of dizzying export growth ___(1)___ (begin) once the reformist camp reaffirmed its authority over economic policy in the early 1990s. Deng, in one of the final political gambits of his career, ___(2)___ (launch) his famous "southern tour" in 1992 to focus national attention on the successes of earlier policy experiments in a handful of locations on China's east coast. These efforts ___(3)___ (include) the creation of special economic zones (SEZs), which allowed foreign companies to set up factories that imported inputs and exported final outputs, relatively free from the interference of government minders. As reformers ___(4)___ (retake) the helm, China embraced global markets more fully, ___(5)___ (push) the number of SEZs from 20 in 1991 to 150 in 2010. According to the World Bank, inflows of foreign direct investment, which ___(6)___ (average) only 0.7% of GDP during the 1980s, surged to 4.2% of GDP during the 1990s and 2000s. Production for foreign markets began a spectacular ascent, with China's share of world manufacturing exports ___(7)___ (grow) from 2.3% in 1991 to 18.8% in 2013. To provide context for China's reintegration into the world economy, we ___(8)___ (highlight) key aspects of its recent performance that inform the analysis of attendant labor-market outcomes in developed Countries.

练习3：将下列研究问题转化为描述研究目的的表达

例：

> **Research Question**: Is there any effect of using computer-assisted instruction compared to a lecture-discussion technique in teaching principles? (explore)
>
> **The statement of Purpose**: In this study, we try to explore the potential effect of using computer-assisted instruction compared to a lecture-discussion technique in teaching principles.

(1) **Research Question**: Are there any influences of agricultural soil management on soil microbiological composition and abundance? (identify)

The aim of this study was _____
_____

(2) **Research Question**: Will farmer characteristics and contextual environmental factors lead to good or bad credit for farmers? (determine)

This study seeks to _____
_____

第6章　描述研究方法

本章将介绍 SSCI 论文的"研究方法 (Methodology)"部分。从图 6-1 可以看出，这个部分在论文中位于"引言（Introduction）"与"结果（Results）"之间。

SSCI 论文中，虽然"研究方法"部分在不同的专业领域会有不同的标题名称见表 6-1，但作用都是用以具体详细地描述本研究的研究过程。作者的写作思路一般基于对以下两个问题的回答：①自己使用了什么？（What did we use/adopt？）②自己是如何做的？（How did we proceed？）在阅读论文的"研究方法"部分时，了解作者的写作思路有助于读者尽快熟悉他们的研究过程和使用的方法。

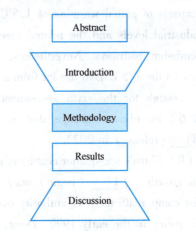

图 6-1　"研究方法"在论文主体中的位置

表 6-1　"研究方法"部分的名称举例

序号	论文标题	发表时间	期刊	"研究方法"部分名称
1	Finance, law and poverty: Evidence from India	2020	Journal of Corporate Finance	Data, methodology, and summary statistics
2	A benchmark of machine learning approaches for credit score prediction	2021	Expert Systems With Applications	The proposed benchmark methodology
3	Heterogeneous choice in the demand for agriculture credit in China: results from an in-the field choice experiment	2020	China Agricultural Economic Review	Experiment implementation and data description
4	Can media and text analytics provide insights into labour market conditions in China?	2019	International Journal of Forecasting	Methodology
5	Analysis of spatial variability in factors contributing to vegetation restoration in Yan'an, China	2020	Ecological Indicators	Materials and methods

6.1　研究方法的重要性

"研究方法"是 SSCI 论文主体的必要组成部分，原因如下：

一是科研成果必须是可重复的（replicable）——保证同行在必要时能根据"研究方法"部分的描述完成和验证作者的研究过程，以得到相同的研究结果。

二是期刊审稿人重点关注本章节——从

审稿人视角出发，常常根据作者提供的研究方法来判断研究结果的可靠性（reliability）和有效性（validity）。

具体到经济和管理学科的实证研究，要以一定的理论及模型作为基础，然后通过具体的数据收集和分析来实现研究结果的有效性和可靠性，步骤如下：

（1）建立计量模型

计量模型一般根据本研究依据的理论基础或模型推导而出，以对本研究中变量之间的因果关系做出判断，建立相应的回归方程等。

（2）选择计量方法

建立了计量模型和获取数据后，即可根据数据的特征和分类选择计量方法。例如，解释一般性数据，通常先对数据进行 OLS㊀ 分析，然后画残差图，大体观察扰动项是否符合经典假设，随后进行严格检验。如果结果出现违背（如异方差），再通过稳健标准误估计量等方式进行处理。（陈强[12]）

（3）解释回归结果

通过计算机软件（如 Stata）等获得的计量结果需要进行进一步的提取和分析，以获取本研究需要的数据。

（4）诊断性及稳健性检验

在估计完模型后，应对计量方法的前提条件或结论的可靠性进行诊断性检验，即"稳健性检验（robustness test）"。稳健性检验考察的就是评价方法和指标解释能力的强壮性。当改变了一些条件或者假设发现所得结论依然不变，那么研究的结论就是稳健的，反之，若所得结论有待商榷，则需要找出使结论发生改变的原因并进行解释。

6.2 研究方法的信息要素

由于具体研究方法和过程的差异，SSCI 论文的"研究方法"部分包含的信息要素呈现多样化特征。但一般都包含以下几个基本要素，见表 6-2。在一些研究领域中，作者会把整个内容分成若干个小节，用加小标题的方式分别描述。

表 6-2 "研究方法"的信息要素

要素名称	要素名称（英文）	具体功能
1. 研究设计（可选）	Research/Study Design	呈现本研究设计的总体框架
2. 研究对象（必选）	Population/Subjects/Participants/Variables etc.	描述样本来源，如规模、收集的位置、特征等
		采样方法与收集过程
		样本的限制条件
3. 建模或研究方法（必选）	Model/Equation/System etc.	描述所建模型、公式及体系及适用性；阐述所选研究方法与研究问题的适恰性
4. 数据收集（必选）	Data (Collection)	介绍数据来源
		描述数据收集方法及采用的原因
5. 研究过程（必选）	The Procedure	介绍研究步骤
	Statistical Analysis	数据的描述性统计和实证过程的分析

㊀ OLS：Ordinary Least Squares，普通最小二乘法。是回归分析（Regression Analysis）最根本的一个形式，对模型条件要求最少，也就是使散点图上的所有观测值到回归直线距离的平方和最小。

6.3 研究方法的语言特征

6.3.1 描述模型

（1）初次介绍模型时，一般使用以下句型对采用的模型及模型的功能进行介绍见表6-3。时态上多采用一般时态（现在时或过去时）来陈述该事实。

由于模型的使用建立在一定的前提条件下，作者一般会对这些条件进行说明，此处的常用句型为

表6-3 "介绍模型"的句法结构和时态特征示例

主语	动词	模型（系统）名称	从句或分句引导词	从（分）句描述模型内容
We	employ	a stylized model	incorporating	information frictions over the cost and benefits of an insurance program
We	present	a stylized model	that	outlines the main mechanisms for our empirical analysis
We	start with	a simple model	that	captures the key considerations in firms' expansion decision
This study/paper	developed	a systematic and comprehensive LFRI system	from	administrative, economic, social, and ecological perspectives to evaluate LF (Land Finance) risks

- We assume that the decision of how many new outlets to open depends on the revenue and cost associated with the additions.
- We assume that an individual decision to consume is as a result of utility maximisation subject to a budget constraint.
- Assumptions are added to the model to characterize a heterogeneous treatment effect, in which the treatment effect varies with price, and the welfare impact of reducing information frictions.

（2）对已有模型进行的改进。如果采用的模型不是原创模型，而是对已有模型的改进，写作时应做以下说明：

- The model, which draws inspiration from *Einav et al.*（2010）and *Handel et al.*（2019）, starts from the individual participation decision, to characterize how providing information on the costs（premium）and benefits（coverage）introduces heterogeneity in the response to the information intervention.
- We build on the structural credit risk model of *Leland and Toft*（1996）by adding an illiquid secondary bond market. This setting is generic and applies to both financial and nonfinancial firms, although the effects illustrated by our model are stronger for financial firms due to their higher leverage and shorter debt maturities.
- We follow *Ecker and Qaim*（2011）and more recently *Hoang*（2018）, and employ a Working-Leser model to study the allocation of household food and non-food expenditure as follows.

上述例子可以看出，如果该模型是基于已有模型的改进，作者要对此进行说明，说明的方法是先说明模型的来源（模型名称+引用来源），再简要说明引用和改进该模型在本研究中的作用。

（3）描述公式。在介绍模型的过程中，

一般要对使用的公式进行介绍，主要是对公式服务的对象及公式中的变量进行描述。此部分的语言表达比较固定，请看下面的例子：

例 6.1（AE 9）

> The administrative, economic, social, ecological, and total risk scores of LF are calculated as:
>
> $$RiskScore = \frac{\sum(w_j^* \times x_j)}{\sum w_j^*} \quad (1)$$
>
> where w_j^* is the weight of indicator j, ranging from 0 to 1; x_j is the normalised data, ranging from 0 to 100; and the range of j corresponds to the number of indicators contained by each sub-risks and total risk.

例 6.2（AE 20）

> Consider a firm. Suppose that, in the absence of leverage, the firm's asset value $\{V_t: 0 \leq t < \infty\}$ follows a geometric Brownian motion in the risk-neutral probability measure
>
> $$\frac{dV_t}{V_t} = (r-\delta)dt + \sigma dZ_t, \quad (1)$$
>
> where r is the constant risk-free rate, δ is the firm's constant cash payout rate, σ is the constant asset volatility, and $\{Z_t: 0 \leq t < \infty\}$ is a standard Brownian motion, representing random shocks to the firm's fundamental. Throughout the paper, we refer to V_t as the firm's fundamental.

对此类信息结构的句法特征可以总结为表 6-4。

表 6-4 "描述公式"的句法特征和时态示例

要计算的变量	动词词组	公式	对单个符号解释
The economic and total risk scores of LF	are calculated as	—	where	h is the... condition, and x is a group of... that affect...
Firm i's (expected) revenue (Rit) from its stores	is formulated as	—	
The expression of the determinants of health	can be expressed as	—	

在介绍公式时，作者一般会给出论文的基本假设，这里的常用句型为

- We assume that the decision of how many new outlets to open depends on the revenue and cost associated with the additions.

- We assume that an individual decision to consume is as a result of utility maximization subject to a budget constraint.

- Assumptions are added to the model to characterize a heterogeneous treatment effect, in which the treatment effect varies with price, and the welfare impact of reducing information frictions.

6.3.2 描述数据的采集和分析

在描述数据收集或研究过程时，完成这些步骤的主体是作者自己，因此描述的重点为方法或步骤，因此在语态方面多采用被动语态。

例 6.3（AE 15）

> The data on political leaders are drawn from the China Political Elite Database (CPED). For each leader, the database provides standardized information about the

> time, place, organization, and rank of every job assignment listed in his or her curriculum vitae (CV), which is collected from government websites, yearbooks, and other trustworthy internet sources. We match each city-year spell in the panel dataset with a city secretary and a mayor. In cases where multiple leaders hold the same post within a given spell, the person with the longest tenure is chosen.

例 6.4（AE 10）

> With the Landsat 5 TM images in 1999 and 2010 as data sources, the land use database update method is used to manually interpret land use maps on the ArcGIS 10.2 platform. First of all, land use map in 2010 (1:10,000) can be directly obtained from Yan'an land use database. If change is found between the two years' images in a polygon in the land use map of 2010, land use type will be updated for the new land use map for 1999; if not, the land use type in 1999 will be the same as that of 2010. Finally, the land use maps are converted to grid layers (Fig. 2).

由于在描述数据收集过程中往往包含多个步骤，因此在写作过程中要尽量避免使用重复的句法结构或相同的词组，以免给读者留下单一刻板的印象。例 6.5 给我们提供了一个句子选择多样化的示范：

例 6.5（AE 23）

> The data for this part of the analysis comes from three sources.
> First, we use geo-spatial data from the World Bank Urban Development Unit to identify the coordinates of the GQ/NS-EW corridor.
> Second, we use geo-spatial data from DIVA-GIS to match Indian districts with the GQ/NS-EW corridor.
> Third, data regarding the individual sections that make up the GQ/NS-EW corridor comes from annual reports of the National Highway Authority of India (NHAI).

读者也可以回到例 6.1 和例 6.2，看作者在表达单个变量时，选用动词的多样化。

课外拓展与练习

★ **学术知识小课堂**

社会科学研究方法的信度与效度

社会科学研究的一个重要特征就是对人类行为的量化。这种量化过程多基于实证主义观点和经验分析方法（Smallbone & Quinton[13]）。

一、效度/有效性（Validity）

实证研究中的效度/有效性是指一个概念被准确描述的程度（Heale & Twycross[14]）。例如，我们要从实证研究的角度论证"左撇子的人更聪明"这个命题是否成立，就需要找到用手习惯与智商之间的相关性了。此类研究的第一步，就是如何界定"左撇子（left-handers）"的概念。在此类研究用手习惯与人类活动的论文中，我们都可以看到作者对"用手倾向（handedness）"分类的介绍，以确保研究数据的效度。

关于效度如何分类，学界有不同的认识。这里介绍的分类是根据 DROST[15] 专门针对社会科学研究的四大分类。

1. 统计结论效度（Statistical Conclusion Validity）

统计结论效度是检验研究结果的数据分析程序与方法的有效性的指标。统计结论效度的基本问题是两个变量之间是否有显著的统计关系。

2. 内部效度（Internal Validity）

内部效度用于判断一项研究的自变量与因变量之间关系的明确程度。如果自变量和因变量之间关系并不会由于其他变量的存在受到影响，那么这项研究就具有较高的内部效度。

3. 构思效度（Construct Validity）

构思效度又称“构想效度”或“结构效度”。牛津字典对“construct”一词的基本解释为“an idea or belief that is based on various pieces of evidence which are not always true（根据不总是真实的各种证据得出的）构想、观念和概念”。这里的“construct”一词主要针对在人类行为研究或心理学研究中那些抽象的，假设性的概念、特性或变量，如智力、创造力、焦虑、动机等。这些抽象的要素很难简单量化并准确测量。构思效度就是测量理论上的构想或特质程度，即测验的结果是否能证实或解释某一理论的假设或构想。

4. 外部效度（External Validity）

外部效度是因变量与自变量之间关系的推广性程度，涉及研究结论的概括力和外推力。

外部效度通常要回答的问题是研究结果是否具有代表性？在类似情境中能否验证研究结果？最后，我们需要知道效度的检验是逐步展开的。研究者可以通过在不同的阶段提出不同的问题来检验一项研究的各等级效度。

二、信度/可靠性（Reliability）

实证研究中的“信度”也称“可靠性”，是指采用同样的方法对同一对象重复测量时所得结果的一致性程度。

在这篇题为“基于主成分分析法的职业经理人创新能力提升影响因素分析[16]”的论文中，研究者建立量表，试图从知识、服务、行为和变革四个维度分析某大型国企职业经理人的创新能力。如图 6-2 所示。

49

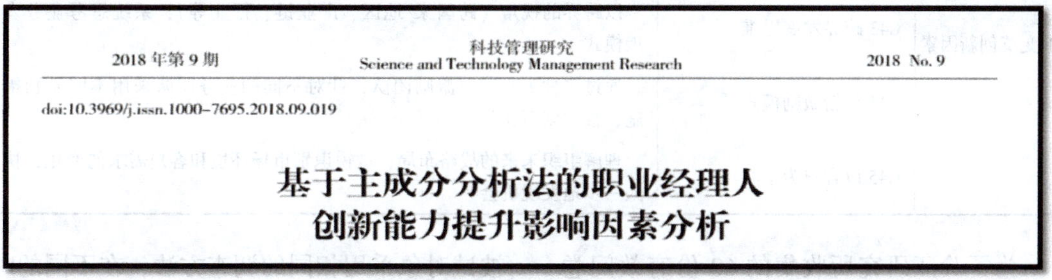
2018 年第 9 期 科技管理研究 Science and Technology Management Research 2018 No. 9

doi:10.3969/j.issn.1000-7695.2018.09.019

基于主成分分析法的职业经理人创新能力提升影响因素分析

图 6-2 示例论文基本信息

表 6-5 量表的相应指标解释

因　子	测 量 指 标	指 标 含 义
C1 知识创新因素	C11 持续学习新知识	变“要我学习”为“我要学习”，在实践中不断学习并提升技能
	C12 开放接纳新思想	对新观点、新思想、新技术持开放态度，对他人创新行为给予认可鼓励，容忍和接受创新失败
	C13 融入学习型组织	善于从组织共享环境下构建或融入多形式的学习组织，具有知识共享意识
	C14 发现并改进薄弱环节	抓住细节，时刻质疑当前采用的技术流程工艺的效能，并提出改进建议
	C15 探寻解决问题新方法	处理问题时能尝试采用不同的新方法，能从多角度，多维度分析解决问题

(续)

因　子	测量指标	指标含义
C2 服务创新因素	C21 凝聚组织战斗力	以身作则，加强业务沟通，促进团队成员之间信任与互赖，形成团队合力
	C22 营造协同协作环境	以价值增值为目标，通过系统分析规划，促进资源在跨团队、跨部门或跨业务的共享
	C23 构建高效团队	完善管理机制、提升组织能力，带领和激励人才，获得团队支持信任
	C24 激发组织活力	打破所辖组织管理边界，重新设计组织运营模式，建立高效的无边界组织
	C25 个人情绪控制	能控制自己的情绪、团队的情绪，为团队提振信心
C3 行为创新因素	C31 制定计划和把握要点	能够不折不扣的落实团队计划、临时性任务，把握工作计划的重要节点
	C32 执行突破力	勇于挑战自我，敢于迎难而上，善于采取各种方法突破瓶颈，攻克难关
	C33 善于整合资源	主动搜寻挖掘内外部优质资源，进行有机整合，高效配置，促进协同
	C34 敢于激情奉献	将自身价值实现与组织事业紧密相连，具有强烈的事业心和使命感，以执着和激情感染他人
	C35 突发事件应急处置	有突发事件的处置能力，对突发应急事件能当机立断采取创新思路来解决
C4 变革创新因素	C41 把握全局观念	跳出所辖领域，站在更高层级或更大的市场看问题，对其他领域工作的合理发展建议
	C42 战略管理思维	系统思考业务发展趋势，把握行业发展规律，前瞻性预判潜在机会
	C43 跨界发展思维	以跨界的视角（跨国家/地区、产业链、行业等），系统思考业务发展模式
	C44 创新激励模式	通过多种手段感召激励团队，针对不同的业务团队采用不同激励措施，推动创新变革
	C45 以客户为中心	理解组织未来的战略布局，敏锐识别市场环境和客户需求的变化，快人一步地发现机会

为了验证研究所收集的 60 份有效问卷结果是否能反映该企业整体的职业经理人情况，研究者选用著名的克朗巴哈系数来检验量表的信度。经过对数据采用 SPSS 统计软件的分析，四个维度的克朗巴哈系数都超过 0.7，说明量表的一致性较好，也表明这批问卷数据能代表该企业整体的状况，见表 6-5。

同样，根据 Drost[15]论文中的分类，社会科学研究中的信度分析也可以分为四类。

1. 重测信度（Test-Retest Reliability）

重测信度也称为再测信度，是对同一组被试对象采用相同的调查方法，在不同的时间先后调查两次，两次调查结果之间的差异程度。

2. 复本信度（Parallel-Form Reliability）

复本信度又称等效本信度或等值信度（Alternative-Form），是指用两套具有相似性的测量工具所测结果的相似程度。例如，在问卷调查中，设计两套在难度、长度、排布、内容上尽可能相似的问卷，这两套问卷是等价的，称为复本，用两套问卷调查同一个对象，比较相应问题的答案，求出相关系数。

3. 分半信度（Split-Half Reliability）

分半信度是通过将测验分成两半，计算这两半测验之间的相关性而获得的信度系数。

4. 内部一致性信度（Internal Consistency Reliability）

内部一致性信度又称内部一致性系数，是指用来测量同一个概念的多个计量指标的一致性程度。例如，针对客户的调查问卷中的各题目在多大程度上考察了同一内容。

总之，效度关注测量结果的有效性和正确性；信度主要回答测量结果的一致性和稳定性问题。一般学者都认为，效度是信度的前提，如果没有效度的测量，即使它的信度再高，这样的测量也是没有意义的。信度是效度的必要条件，效度都必须建立在信度的基础上。

★请完成以下练习

练习1：将下列句子表达的信息与对应的语言功能配对

> 1. 描述标准的或之前使用过的方法
> 2. 给出是否选择一种方法的理由
> 3. 介绍使用该方法的目的
> 4. 描述研究对象特征
> 5. 描述研究过程

（1）功能：_____

• To generate a physical map, the BAC library was prepared from … using standard methods.

（2）功能：_____

• We conducted an analysis of X and Y for a broad range of … in order to explore extraction effects on SIA results.

（3）功能：_____

• Initially, X were adjusted to get a reasonable match between simulated and generally observed dates of Y, followed by adjusting several other parameters.

• First of all, land use map in 2010 can be directly obtained from Yan'an land use database, and then to interpret land-use types in 1999 based on the land use map of ….

（4）功能：_____

• Another suitable measure is the G-mean that can be used to evaluate the balance between classification performance in both minority and majority classes.

• Based on the above literature review on the effects of X (Tan et al., 2012; Geng et al., 2018), considering the availability of data, this study developed a systematic and comprehensive LFRI system to evaluate Y risks.

（5）功能：_____

• Hoogenbloom et al (2015) identified several advantages of the case study. …

• The proposed benchmark aims to deal with credit risk prediction problem for supporting investors in the evaluation of ….

练习2：用方框中适当的词填空，以正确描述研究开展的过程

> According to   are shown   Since
> In particular   The aim
> provided by   Finally   using

__(1)__ of our evaluation is to compare several classifications of engines' performances __(2)__ several sampling strategies according to different evaluation metrics. For the proposed analysis we have selected the data-set __(3)__ a real P2P lending platform. __(4)__ Aksakalli (2019), we have considered loan status as target class for our problem, whose values __(5)__ in Table 1. __(6)__ we considered the binary problem if a loan will be paid back, we only take into account the labels "FullyPaid" or "Charged off". __(7)__, we performed a 10-cross validation in which the data set has been divided into a training and test set at ratio 7 : 3 for each step. __(8)__ we have also compared the obtained results with respect to the ones computed in Namvar et al. (2018) and Song et al. (2020) using the same evaluation metrics.

第 7 章　叙述研究结果

本章将介绍如何撰写 SSCI 论文的研究结果（Results）。研究结果在有些论文中独立存在如图 7-1a 所示，而在另一部分论文中是与"讨论（Discussion）"合并为"结果和讨论"部分如图 7-1b 所示，从而对每一个研究结果进行更深入的解释和评价。在本章中，我们会采用图 7-1a 结构的形式，将"研究结果"看作独立部分进行介绍，并在第 8 章详细介绍"讨论（Discussion）"部分的信息要素和语言特征。

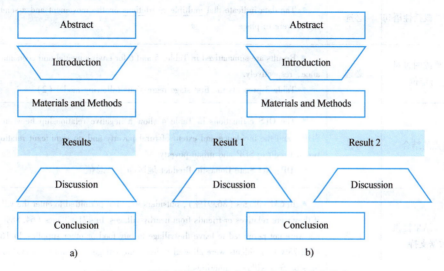

图 7-1　"研究结果"在论文主体中的位置及形式

SSCI 论文的"研究结果"是一篇论文中最主要的呈现原创数据和最新发现的部分。有经验的作者在撰写结果部分时，一定会同时考虑"讨论（Discussion）"的内容。这是因为在"讨论"部分，作者要对"结果"部分呈现的内容进行解释、比较与评价，这两个部分存在必要的逻辑关系。

"结果"部分的信息一般通过**数据**（表格或图表）和**文本**两种形式来呈现。在本章，我们聚焦文本部分的信息要素和语言特征，而"图表与表格"的呈现形式将放在第 10 章介绍。

7.1　研究结果文本部分的信息要素

"研究结果"要呈现的内容，在学科之间差异显著。例如，在一些学科中，"研究结果"部分不允许出现对结果的任何讨论，而有些学科允许对本研究结果进行评价或解释。总体而言，该部分使用文字信息叙述研究结果时，包含以下要素见表 7-1。

表 7-1 "研究结果"的信息要素及排列顺序

信息要素名称	必/可选	举 例
1. 回顾研究问题或方法	可选	• In this section, we examine if there is a significant relationship between financial development and poverty and if it is robust to endogeneity concerns using two instruments for financial development（回顾研究问题）
	可选	• A cluster analysis using both hierarchical and non-hierarchical methods (*Hair et al.*, 2010) was applied to test if firm clusters exist among SMMEs in terms of their levels of implementing eco-innovation（回顾研究方法）
2. 叙述结果的概括性语句	必选	• The data indicate that multiple restrictions on the movement and assembly of villagers were in place
3. 利用表格或图表对结果进行定位	必选	• Results are summarized in Tables 5 and 6 for environmental and economic performance, respectively. • Table 3 presents the first stage regressions following model (2)
第 2、3 点的结合	可选	• The OLS estimations in Table 4 show a negative relationship between Credit to SDP* and the incidence and extent of rural poverty and no significant relationship between Credit to SDP and urban poverty * SDP: Net State Domestic Product 地区净生产总值
4. 对每一项结果提供具体数据支持	必选	• In 631 villages (86.91%), outsiders were not permitted to enter the village, even if they were relatives or friends from nearby villages. In 471 villages (64.88%), villagers were not permitted to leave the village to buy food or other supplies. In 165 villages (22.73%), residents were allowed to leave the village, but were required to have permission from village authorities to do so
5. 对结果进行评价、比较或解释	可选	• This result not only shed light on the difference between the coastal and inland labor market, it also reinforces previous findings that the LMCI* is sensitive to actual labor market development（说明结果意义） * LMCI: Chinese labor market conditions index 劳动力市场条件指数
		• For each of the forecast horizons, our LMCI provides forecasts of credit deviations that are significantly better than those from equations using the official unemployment rate and the manufacturing PMI employment sub-index, as per the Diebold-Mariano test. The forecast from the urban supply-demand ratio and the non-manufacturing PMI employment sub-index beat those of our LMCI, but the improvement in forecast accuracy is not significant（进行解释和比较）

下面，我们通过 AE 23 的 Results 部分节选来看一下这些要素在具体文章中的运用（例 7.1）。

例 7.1（AE 23）

> [1] We begin our empirical analysis with an estimation of the output elasticity of the private factors of production (capital and labor) and public investment for manufacturing firms in the formal and informal sectors. [2] Tables 6 and 7 report the results of regressing firm-level GVA* in each sector on the private and public inputs, along with controls at both the level of the firm and the state, as expressed in (7). [3] Columns 1-3 in each table reports estimates from the OLS, LP-S, and ACF methods, respectively, for the flow specification of public investment, while columns 4-6 report the corresponding results for the stock specification. [4] For public investment, we estimate the output elasticity both for the aggregate measure (development expenditures), as well as its sub-categories (social and economic services). [5] We should note that our focus will be on the estimates from the stock specification of public investment. [6] As Futagami et al. (1993), Glomm and Ravikumar (1994), Turnovsky and Fisher (1995) and others have argued, what is relevant for the productivity of the firm is the accumulated stock of public capital (say, access to roads, power, etc.) rather than the flow of spending on public goods by the government.
>
> *GVA：Gross Value Added 增加值总额；总增加值

- 句1：回顾研究过程
- 句2：总述研究结果
- 句3~4：具体描述结果
- 句5~6：对结果进行解释和比较

7.2 叙述研究结果的语言特征

7.2.1 叙述研究结果的句法特征

当论文作者使用文字叙述研究结果时，叙述的内容可以概括为以下三个方面：

（1）描述变量在某个时间段或范围内的变化见表 7-2。

（2）对不同变量、研究对象或方法进行比较见表 7-3。

表 7-2 描述变化的基本句式结构

变量	表示变化的动词词组	范围/对象/条件
The average effect of assignment to the information intervention	does not change	as base period individual controls and firm-level controls are added in models (2) and (3), respectively
HR slack	increases	Tobin's q by 0.1.
The spatial autocorrelations of the Moran's I values	showed a growing trend	—
LTR, FR, and LTD in China	were all on the rise	during the period of 1998-2017

表 7-3 进行比较的基本句式结构

变量 1	表达比较的动词词组	变量 2
The positive relationship between financial slack and change in human capital investment	is a better metric than	ET itself for visual comparison of daily water use calculations
The negative effect of PM2.5 concentration on public health	was higher than	that without considering the spatial factor
The mean grain size of reaction-derived Fe_3O_4 is 22nm	which is a little bigger than	the measurement with SEM

我们看到,在对不同变量、模型、研究对象等进行比较时,常用形容词比较级。但也有使用最高级形式。如:

Education and Skills Status are the two most significant attributes at 51.99% of information significance.

这些句式往往出现在描述具体研究结果的部分。

(3) 描述两个变量之间的联系或影响见表 7-4。

表 7-4 描述关联性的基本句型结构

变量 1	表达相关性的词组	变量 2
Our proxies for access to both informal and formal financial sources	are significantly associated with	the likelihood of running a microenterprise
The travel time to the nearest financial institution	is negatively related with	the likelihood of running a microenterprise
HR slack	has a negative and statistically significant effect on	Tobin's q in the non-change context ($\beta = -0.151$, $p < .001$)

7.2.2 叙述研究结果的动词时态

叙述研究结果的信息一般聚焦本研究,但所陈述的内容可能特指本研究的具体结果,也有可能是对本研究结果评价和说明进行比较、回顾等。因此"研究结果"部分的时态存在多样性见表 7-5。该部分的时态有时也取决于期刊的要求——部分 SSCI 期刊发表的论文习惯统一使用现在时来陈述结果。

表 7-5 "研究结果"部分的主要时态及功能

时态	信息要素及功能	举例
一般现在时	利用表格或图表对结果进行定位	• Fig. 3 illustrates that LTR, FR, and LTD in China were all on the rise during the period of 1998-2017 • In this study, the increase of EVI from 2000 to 2011 (Fig. 4) is used to indicate vegetation restoration
	呈现研究结果	• The rural road density has a higher and more significant positive effect on vegetation restoration in the northwest (Wuqi) and in the southeast (Yichuan)
	陈述研究现状	• The vegetation restoration is influenced by many factors that are normally divided into natural and human activities (Li et al., 2011)

(续)

时 态	信息要素及功能	举 例
一般过去时	回顾研究方法	• The GWR 4.0 software tool (Nakaya, 2016) was applied to perform the GWR model where Gaussian function was used as a weight function
	呈现研究结果	• It can be seen from Fig. 4 that the vegetation in Yan'an showed an overall improvement trend
完成时	介绍已有研究	• Prior studies have shown that this terminator can be exchanged for other rho-independent terminators without abrogating sRNA-mediated repression
情态动词	对结果进行评价	• This model can provide insights to various agencies, governmental or non-governmental social agencies • Dynamic simulation of the Kcb curve may have guided the economic growth model to these improved management recommendations

7.3 对研究结果的解释说明

在本章一开始我们就提到，在一篇论文中"研究结果（Results）"与"讨论（Discussion）"可能是两个独立存在的部分，也有可能是这两个部分合在一起被称为"结果与讨论（Results and Discussion）"。对于"研究结果（Results）"与"讨论（Discussion）"独立存在的情况，我们依然可以在一些论文的"研究结果"部分看到对结果的说明与评价。那么这个部分的评论与"讨论"部分的评论有什么样的区别与联系呢？

我们先来看一下"研究结果"部分的评论所包含的内容。

1. 对具体结果进行评价

（1）作者指出该研究结果的有效性、稳健性、规范性等。

例 7.2（AE 17）

The greatest difference between the robustness test results and the empirical results above is that some of the variable coefficients, spatial spillover coefficients and their significances were improved or decreased (Table 5). However, the estimation results of the core variables were basically consistent with the above conclusions. This shows that the impact of air pollution on public health effect is reliable and robust.

例 7.3（AE 13）

The LCCTS used the survey question to measure risk attitude, whereas we conducted an incentivized experiment to measure risk attitude with the CATS data. Thus, we carry out Durbin-Wu-Hausman tests between Tables 2 and 3 with respect to columns (4) - (6). We find that the FE estimates are not statistically significant. The results suggest that soliciting risk preference through survey questions is also valid in our study.

（2）作者指出本结果的意义，如统计

学意义等。

例 7.4（AE 14）

> To keep the analysis focused on the nutrition transition, we report the model estimates in the online Appendix and only discuss key results here. For both urban and rural sectors, most of the parameters estimated are statistically significant. The highly significant quadratic term for income（λ）supports the non-linearity of the budget share Engel curve of Indian households for their consumption of various food groups and thus establishes the superiority of QUAIDS over AIDS. The QUAIDS results also signal the importance of correction in zero consumption as the coefficients of the probability density functions（φ）are generally statistically significant.

（3）作者评价本结果是否与研究假设相一致，是否回答了研究问题。

例 7.5（AE 13）

> The results reported in Table 4 are consistent with our prediction. Because the CATS sample is too small to divide into subsamples, we use only the LCCTS data only. Columns（1）-（3）report the estimates for mothers, and columns（4）-（6）report the estimates for fathers. Relative to columns（4）-（6）, the magnitudes of the estimated coefficients on children's gender composition in columns（1）-（3）are bigger. Therefore, the effect of children's gender composition on risk attitude is greater for mothers than fathers. The results support our hypothesis on the insurance motive for son preference.

2. 作者对本次研究结果与其他研究者之前的研究结果进行比较

例 7.6（AE 14）

> These estimates indicate that although food remains a necessity, its importance within the household budget in both rural and urban India has declined. These results are consistent with the observation of Deaton and Dreze（2009）who report limited real change in per capita expenditure on food in spite of the rising MPCE*.
>
> *MPCE：Monthly Per Capita Expenditure 月人均支出

3. 作者解释产生该研究结果的原因

例 7.7（AE 3）

> Due to the proximity to manufacturers of specialized hardware and access to cheap electricity, majority of the mining process has been conducted in China as miners in the country account for more than 75% of the Bitcoin network's hashing power, as shown in Fig. 1.

从上述例子我们可以看出，在"研究结果"部分出现的讨论或评论主要是针对具体研究结果的说明和评价。如果是与他人研究做比较，只说明结果一致或存在差异，一般不去展开解释产生差异的原因。而"讨论"部分的讨论或评论会具体解释产生差异的原因，并且往往将研究结果看作一个整体进行综合评价，并基于具体的研究结果展望研究前景。具体的"讨论"内容和框架我们会在第 8 章进行详细介绍。

最后，通过例 7.8 整体了解如何使用文字对"研究结果"进行陈述及对结果进行"适当"的说明与评价。

例 7.8（AE 14）

¹Next, we look at standard demand elasticities in columns (3) and (4). ²While these estimates also confirm to Engel's law and demand theory, they display more variation than the preference-based estimates. ³From 1987-1988 to 2011-2012, the rural and urban standard YED*s decreased from 0.727 to 0.651 and 0.822 to 0.717, respectively, indicating that the proportion of additional income allocated to food expenditure decreases as income increases. ⁴In both sectors, the demand for food has become more sensitive to changes in food price as suggested by the rising trend of PED*. ⁵Thus, these estimates indicate that although food remains a necessity, its importance within the household budget in both rural and urban India has declined. ⁶These results are consistent with the observation of Deaton and Dreze (2009) who report limited real change in per capita expenditure on food in spite of the rising MPCE. ⁷As shown by the trend of standard YED, the rise in total expenditure of Indian households triggers a less than proportional increase in expenditure on food and the magnitude of the increase tends to fall over time. ⁸Deaton and Dreze (2009) also show that the real price of calories increased from 1987-1988 to 1999-2000. ⁹The estimates of PED suggest that the increase in calorie prices causes a rising negative substitution effect* over time, making it more likely to cancel out the falling positive income effect* and leaving the real food expenditure unchanged.

　*YED：the expenditure elasticity (YED) for cereals 购买弹性

　PED：Price Elasticity of Demand 需求价格弹性

　negative substitution effect 负替代效应

　positive income effect 正收入效应

句1~2：总述研究结果

句3~5：描述具体结果

句6~8：对比与评价

句9：指出本结果意义

课外拓展与练习

★学术知识小课堂

介绍"研究结果"的明星词汇——respectively

在介绍研究结果时，论文作者需要对研究发现进行详细说明。这个过程往往体现在一个句子中对同类变量或因子的并列陈述。为了让句子结构更加紧凑并便于读者理解，论文中常使用副词"respectively"来表示"分别的、依次的"。请看下面的例子：

- When PM2.5 concentration increased by one percent, the number of people receiving treatment in hospitals per ten thousand (Y1_

RT), the number of health examinations in hospitals per ten thousand (Y2_HE), and the number of in-patient stays per ten thousand (Y3_HN) increased by 0.398, 0.466, and 0.380%, **respectively**.

上句中论文作者分别对当PM2.5浓度增加1%,每万人在医院接受治疗的人数(Y1_RT)、每万人在医院接受健康检查的人数(Y2_HE)和每万人住院的人数(Y3_HN)三个变量**分别**的增加量(0.398%、0.466%和0.380%)进行陈述。

要正确使用"respectively",应注意以下几点:

(1) 当一个句子中存在两组或多组并列的信息列举时,要确保每一组列举在随后有具体的信息内容一一对应,才可以使用"respectively"而不引起歧义。

• We performed under-identification tests and weak-identification tests to verify the validity of the instrumental variable and critical value respectively. (×)

• We performed the under-identification test to verify the validity of the instrumental variable and critical value, respectively. (√)

• To verify the validity of the instrumental variable and critical value, we performed both under-identification tests and weak-identification tests. (√)

(2) 当一个句子中描述一个主题,并随后针对这项主题进行两组支撑信息列举时,并不需要使用"respectively"。

• The coefficient on homeownership in the column is positive and significant and lies between 3.84 and 3.87 percentage points, respectively. (×)

• The coefficient on homeownership in the column is positive and significant and lies between 3.84 and 3.87 percentage points. (√)

(3) 句中的"respectively"后或句末的"respectively"前一般使用逗号",",强调在respectively处并列信息的存在,以使句子表达更清晰。

We control for provincial fixed effects, γp to account for permanent differences across provinces and include year dummies, τt to account for time-varying national determinants of homeownership and wellbeing. a0 and εit are respectively, the constant and error term in the model. (√)

*, ** and *** indicate significance at the 10%, 5% and 1% levels, respectively. (√)

当然,除了"respectively"之外,论文作者在"研究结果"部分也会使用其他表示"可能性"或"相关性"的副词来强化信息之间的逻辑性,请看下面的例子:

• **Similarly**, for children of locals there is a significant and positive effect of homeownership on their subjective wellbeing, while homeownership has an insignificant effect on the SWB of children of migrants.

• **Ideally**, to attribute a causal interpretation to the effects one would utilize a valid external instrumental variable (IV) which is correlated with homeownership, but is not correlated with the child's SWB except via their parents' homeownership status.

• Columns (1)-(3) show that the travel time to the nearest financial institution is negatively related with the likelihood of running a microenterprise. **Specifically**, a 10% lower travel time to the nearest financial institution is associated with a 6% higher likelihood of running a microenterprise.

• Using quantile regressions, we show that while the productivity benefits of public investment are spread evenly across the size distribution of formal sector firms, they are strictly increasing in firm size for the informal sector. **Additionally**, smaller informal firms are significantly disadvantaged by the highway upgrades: public investment benefits not only the larger firms in each sector, but also formal firms much more than informal ones.

• **Presumably**, the inter-annual fluctuation of the growth rates of LTR and LTD have been similar but different from that of FR (Fig. 4).

★请完成以下练习

练习1：找出三篇与你的研究方向高度相关的文章，阅读其"研究结果"部分。按照下表"示例文章"对信息要素的统计方式分析自选文章的信息要素并填写表格

信息要素	示例文章	自选文章1	自选文章2	自选文章3
1. 回顾研究问题/目的/方法	（句1）... a full sample estimation with spatial factors was performed for this paper			
2. 总体叙述研究结果	（句3）It can be seen from the table that the regression estimation with spatial factors was more significant			
3. 利用表格或图表对结果进行定位	（句2）Table 3 shows the results of the full sample estimates for public health when considering ...			
第2、3的结合	—			
4. 对每一项结果提供具体数据支持	（句4）The R^2 values of the two models ... were 0.78, and the R^2 values of the other models exceeded 0.8, which were higher than ... （句5）the LogL value was higher than that ...			
5. 对结果进行评价，比较或解释	（句6）the public health regression model considering spatial factors was more effective			

示例文章（AE 17）：

^{1}Due to the existence of the spatial effect, a full sample estimation with spatial factors was performed for this paper. ^{2}Table 3 shows the results of the full sample estimates for public health when considering spatial factors. ^{3}It can be seen from the table that the regression estimation with spatial factors was more significant. ^{4}The R^2 values of the two models along the dimension of the number of people receiving treatment in hospitals were 0.78, and the R^2 values of the other models exceeded 0.8, which were higher than that for the model without considering the spatial factors. ^{5}At the same time, the LogL value was higher than that for the model without spatial factors, and the explanatory variables in the model were more significant. ^{6}Therefore, the public health regression model considering spatial factors was more effective.

练习2：将下列句子表达的信息与对应的语言功能配对

1. 解释结果出现的意外和偏差
2. 对研究结果进行评价
3. 对研究结果进行总结
4. 通过表格或图表说明研究结果

(1) 功能：_____

• Taken together, these results suggest that...

• In general, these findings suggest that there is a binding between...

(2) 功能：_____

• Finally, a digital map (Fig. 4) of... is drawn, with guiding principle to optimize.

• Each critical value of the t-statistic generates a two-by-two table like Table 1, from which we can compute...

• From Table 3, all the four zoning methods have achieved...

(3) 功能：_____

• The difference between... and ... was not statistically significant.

• ... remains marginally insignificant.

• A very small F-ratio (< 0.1) means that the difference between groups is significant.

(4) 功能：_____

• The discrepancy with the data might be due to the fact that...

• The difference can be attributed to the misuse of...

• The inconsistency is probably the consequence of a relatively small sample...

练习3：将括号中的词汇重新进行排列，以便更合理地描述研究结果

例如：

• (shown/as/Fig. 1a/in), as the temperature increased above 60 C, (also/between/the/difference/increased/ the Dirac distribution and Fld distribution).

• <u>As shown in Fig. 1</u>, as the temperature increased above 60 C, <u>the difference between the Dirac distribution and Fld distribution also increased</u>.

(1) (that/Fig. 3a/shows) access to informal and formal financial services is (for the microenterprises/also/the size of the initial investment/important for).

(2) (be/in/Fig. 3d/observed/it/that/can) the coefficients of (are/shares of/consumed/outside/ meals/ the home/significant) and negative.

(3) (give/ (2) /columns (1) /and) the preference-based elasticities, which are (using/computed 2017-2018/in/the mean data point).

(4) (from/as/Figs. 2 and 3/seen), Moran's I increased from 0.231 to 0.277 during 2004-2013, which (the local autocorrelation/of/indicates/Y1_RT/that) had been enhanced in China.

(5) (Table 2/the estimated results/in/in/comparison with), we can see that (PM2.5/the negative effect/concentration/of/ public health/ on) was higher than (considering/ without / that/the spatial factor).

练习4：用方框中所给副词填空

| effectively | arbitrarily |
| additionally | not surprisingly |

(1) This indicates an inverted U-shaped relationship between mayors' tenure and firm pollution discharge. ____, the coefficient of Education is positive and passes the 1% significance test.

(2) The first scenario is to ____ delete 6 farmers for each creditworthiness level from the generator group.

(3) Turning to the control variables, we note that —____— households in urban areas are more likely to run a microenterprise.

(4) Advanced functionality can ____ evaluate farmer creditworthiness.

第 8 章　讨论与结论

SSCI 论文的"讨论（Discussion）"部分在向读者、审稿人和期刊编审等阅读对象展示作者研究的创新性和学术贡献等方面发挥着重要作用，是论文主体不可或缺的一部分。我们先来看一下"讨论"部分在论文中的位置。

例 8.1（AE 6）

在这篇名为"When a son is born: The impact of fertility patterns on family finance in rural China"的论文中，"Discussion（讨论）"作为论文的第四部分"Results（研究结果）"的一个小章节存在。这种结构代表了一部分 SSCI 论文"Discussion（讨论）"在论文中的位置。本文具体的结构如图 8-1 所示。

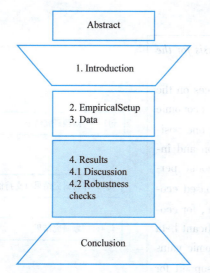

图 8-1　"Discussion（讨论）"部分在论文中的位置示例

例 8.2（AE 16）

> 5. Results and Discussion
> 5.1. *Relationships between creditworthiness level, farmer characteristics and contextual factors*
>
> The generated rules can provide insights to relationships of creditworthiness and various contextual and farmer characteristics. These rules show a number of possible evaluation strategies that can identify creditworthiness level. It would be helpful to decision makers to delineate the relationship between farmers' characteristics, environmental factors, and creditworthiness. There were 13,774 rules generated. This large set of rules can help develop a rule base which be used to predict the creditworthiness level of farmers. The rule base can be updated over time as new farmer samples are introduced.

例 8.2 的论文标题为"Banking creditworthiness: Evaluating the complex relationships"。这篇论文的"讨论（Discussion）"部分与"研究结果（Results）"合并为一个板块，称为"Results and Discussion（结果与讨论）"如图 8-2 所示。这种结构中往往有若干个"研究结果（Results）"并存，作者会以小标题的形式分别给出每一项具体的结果与针对本结果的讨论。之后会有一个独立的"结论（Conclusion）"部分对全文进行总结。

鉴于在第 7 章已经对"结果（Results）"部分进行了探讨，本章内容将专门针对"讨论"部分的信息及语言特征展开分析。

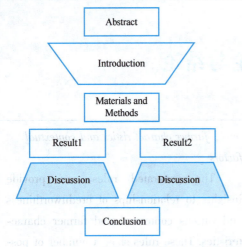

图 8-2 "Discussion（讨论）"部分在论文中位置示例

论文作者在撰写这部分时，会从研究的价值和重要性出发，逐步扩展到基于本研究的研究展望。Weissberg & Buker[6] 将科技论文"讨论"的信息要素分为两部分——**初始（first）信息**和**后续（later）信息**。"初始信息"的信息要素针对本研究结果展开的解释与评价。具体见表 8-1。

表 8-1 "讨论"部分的初始信息要素

针对具体的研究结果
1. 对本研究进行回顾（以下选项可选） • 本研究的主要目标 • 本研究的研究假设 • 本研究的主要结果 • 本研究的研究意义
2. 对本研究最重要的研究结果进行陈述 • 基于研究结果展开评价（以下选项可选） （1）研究结果是否实现研究目标 （2）研究结果是否支持研究假设 （3）研究结果如何服务于本研究的主要活动 （4）研究结果是否回答研究问题 • 评价研究结果与前人研究一致或相反
3. 引用相关文献或对研究结果潜在影响进行阐释

8.1 "讨论"部分的信息要素

SSCI 论文的"讨论"部分主要围绕论文研究结果的意义展开。具体而言，是对作者在"引言（Introduction）"中提出的研究问题和在结果中呈现的研究发现进行充分的解释、比较及评价。

例 8.3（AE 2）

5.1.3. *Discussion on hierarchical regression* analysis for the test of Hypothesis 3*

[1]Table 6 shows the moderating effect of TEM practices on the relationship of eco-innovation practices with economic performance. [2]For eco-innovation planners in Cluster 1, one positive interaction beta shows that technology eco-innovation and internal source reduction (ISR) can jointly improve economic performance. [3]Hypothesis 3 is supported for a technology-based eco-innovation with a specific strengthening factor. [4]However, for eco-innovation adopters in Cluster 2, one negative and significant beta of interaction effect indicates that ISR can weaken economic gains through technology innovation. [5]This result provides no support for Hypothesis 3, which may be attributable to the high level of implementing both ISR and technology innovation. [6]Such a result indicates that when ISR and technology innovation practices are implemented at a certain high level, the marginal benefit can be trivial to cover the marginal cost incurred, resulting in negative economic gain.

* hierarchical regression 层次回归分析

句1~2：回顾研究结果

句3：评价研究结果（支持假设）

句4：回顾研究结果

句5：评价研究结果（不支持假设）

句6：进一步评价研究结果

例 8.4 （AE 1）

[1]Our data show that local governments and village officials across China implemented strict control measures over the movements of residents. [2]Although causality cannot be assigned from our study, the disease prevention policies coincided with the limited spread of the novel coronavirus in China's rural areas and likely helped to contain the infection. [3]This is consistent with recent studies that found that quarantine and travel restrictions effectively reduced the transmission of the virus in China (Leung et al., 2020; Li et al., 2020b).

句1~2：回顾研究结果

句3：评价研究结果

"后续信息"在论文中常常以"（future) implications（应用及展望）"呈现。作者会开始引导读者看到更宏观层面的研究意义，即基于本研究的结果对该领域发展的重要性及对其他研究人员的启发性等，同时部分文章会在此处说明本研究存在的不足见表8-2。

表 8-2 "讨论"部分的后续信息要素

关于研究展望的一般信息
4. 说明本研究的局限性 • 受到研究条件限制产生的例外情况 • 未解决的问题 • 相关性的欠缺等
5. 介绍本研究在理论和实践方面的应用
6. 展望本研究的研究前景

例 8.5 （AE 3）

[1]At the same time, we acknowledge there exists some limitations to our study and outline future directions for research. (limitations omitted) [2]While it is true the blockchain* technology, and Bitcoin* as one of its applications, is, and increasingly will play a significant role in the economy, ultimately, the choice of adopting and using this technology lies in the hands of humans. [3]Consequently, we should carefully evaluate the trade-offs before applying this promising technology to a variety of industries.

* blockchain 区块链　Bitcoin 比特币

句1：说明研究局限性

句2：介绍研究应用

句3：展望研究前景

例8.6 (AE 10)

> 5.2. *Existing inadequacies and outlook*
>
> [1]In this study, both OLS* and GWR* models were applied to analyze the factors contributing to vegetation restoration in Yan'an, China, and it was found that the latter could provide more useful information for policy-makers. [2]However, due to the limitation of data source and data accuracy, the following inadequacies may exist. (limitations omitted) [3]In the future, it may be considered to use the spatial and temporal adaptive reflectance fusion model, which can guarantee both temporal and spatial resolution (Zhu et al., 2010), to improve the accuracy of the vegetation coverage data.
>
> * OLS：Ordinary Least Squares regression 最小二乘法
> GWR：Geographically weighted regression 地理加权回归

句1：回顾研究方法
句2：说明研究局限性
句3：展望研究前景

8.2 "讨论"部分的语言特征

从语言功能上来看，"讨论"部分是对研究结果的解释与评价。为了呈现客观性，作者在语言选择上会持谨慎态度，多选择能够表达中立立场的词句。此部分信息还常带有对本研究结果的不确定性及局限性的探讨，时态上也会呈现多样性。

8.2.1 "讨论"部分的句法特征

由于在"讨论"部分要表明自己的观点，作者在写作中会倾向选择复杂句（complex sentence）结构——以主句（main clause）来呈现自己的观点和立场，并以名词从句（noun clause）来承载具体的信息，见表8-3。

例8.7 (AE 15)

> Interestingly, our estimates indicate that the distributive bias* does not become noticeably larger when more corrupt patrons* or localities are involved. While these results certainly cannot fully rule out the presence of corrupt motives in transfer allocation, they do seem to suggest that the magnitude of patronage-based favoritism* does not merely reflect the level of corruption in a province.
>
> * distributive bias 分配偏差　patron 赞助人，资助者　the magnitude of patronage-based favoritism 基于互惠的偏袒程度

表8-3 "讨论"部分作者的立场与信息

主句（作者立场）	动词		从句（具体信息）
our estimates	indicate	that	the distributive bias does not become noticeably larger when more corrupt patrons* or localities are involved
these results	suggest		the magnitude of patronage-based favoritism does not merely reflect the level of corruption in a province

8.2.2 "讨论"部分的动词时态

通过前面对信息要素的学习，我们了解到作者在讨论他们的研究发现和研究前景时，"初始"信息部分针对本研究，内容更具体；"后续"信息部分的讨论针对研究前景，讨论更加广义的内容。要体现表达的不同语气和不同内容，动词及时态的选择是一个重要方面。

如果使用复杂句，作者一般分别在主句和从句两部分来考量动词的选择和应用见表 8-4。

表 8-4 "讨论"部分复合句中动词的使用示例

序号	主句部分			从句部分			信息功能
	主语	主句		从句主语	从句动词	事实信息	
1	We	find evidence	that	financial liberalization	resulted in	inter-state migration towards states with deeper financial systems	回顾研究结果
2	We	proposed		physical decrements	would be	more apparent in speed jobs than in skill jobs	回顾研究假设
3	The evidence of Bitcoin blockchain operation	suggests		new protocols	should be designed and scheduled	in an environmentally friendly manner	评价、解释研究结果
4	We	found		some managers	focused	too much on DIP results	
5	It	remains possible		we	did not capture gender bias	in human capital investments	说明研究局限性
6	Further study	would be needed to determine	if	our observed community changes	influence	labor movement in this system	展现研究前景

8.3 "讨论"部分的引用功能

"讨论"部分是 SSCI 论文继"引言（Introduction）"后出现引用最多的部分。因为在这个部分，论文作者需要通过与其他研究者研究结果的比较，来说明本研究的意义。表 8-5 列出引用的情境以及信息功能。

表 8-5 "讨论"部分引用示例及功能说明

引用示例	引用说明	信息功能
• In a similar vein, use of data quality improvement methods implies specific metrics that are being monitored as well as visible signals to employees that management is monitoring their ability to achieve those metrics（Rungtusanatham, 2001）. We witnessed this phenomenon in our case study • Upon implementing data quality improvement methods, the focal organization realized higher quality data and information, which evoked further use and satisfaction and ultimately improved decision-making, again supporting the Delone and McLean (2003) model for information systems success due to aspects of quality	引用其他研究者的研究结果，体现本研究的相似性	支持本结果可信度

(续)

引用示例	引用说明	信息功能
• It is noticed that the estimated coefficient of the turnover variable is much smaller than those derived from the IV method in Section 4. There is no precise explanation for this discrepancy. Jiang (2017) presented a survey of 255 papers published in top finance journals that rely on the instrumental variable (IV) approach for identifying causal effects. The author observed that the magnitude of the IV estimates is on average nine times of that of their corresponding uninstrumented estimates. Jiang (2017) offered several explanations. One possible cause is due to the use of weak IVs. Angrist and Pischke (2009) argued that weak instruments yield IV estimates that are biased toward their corresponding OLS estimates. For this reason, we performed weak identification tests to verify the validity of the instrumental variable in all regressions (Tables 3-8)	引用相关研究，解释出现该结果的可能原因	解释结果
• Following the placebo study* by Abadie et al. (2010), we construct a distribution of the average treatment effects to determine whether the effect of the city-renaming reform is significant * placebo study：安慰剂对照	引用其他研究者提出的研究方法	支持本研究结果可信度
• To date, the organization investigated in the study has yet to find the optimal level of quality that should be achieved to properly balance program costs with benefits to prevent a diminishing returns effect (Cohen and Levinthal, 1990; Fichman, 2004a; Hollander, 1997). The questions of "how many resources will be needed" and "what level of quality is needed to achieve the decision-making benefits sought" are questions stakeholders within the firm will need to address as DIPs are planned and put into place	引用相关研究成果，评价研究结果	陈述研究局限性讨论研究前景

8.4 SSCI 论文的"结论"部分

"结论（Conclusion）"，顾名思义就是对本研究成果的总结，是 SSCI 论文的必要组成部分。主要的信息要素包括：

（1）陈述研究局限性（可选）；
（2）总结主要的研究工作（可选）；
（3）重述最重要的研究结果及其内涵或对其进行说明（必选）；
（4）说明研究前景（可选）；
（5）介绍可进一步深入的研究方向或具体课题（可选）。

从以上要素分析可以看出，"结论"部分的信息要素与"讨论"部分的要素相似。这是因为，**很多 SSCI 论文将对"研究结果"的讨论放在了结论部分**。因此，我们不对"结论"的信息要素和语言特征再做单独介绍。

值得注意的是，由于篇幅短小且呈现了本研究最主要的成果信息，很多读者在决定是否精读或引用一篇文章前，会首选快速阅读"结论"部分。

课外拓展与练习

★请完成以下练习

练习 1：请用方框中词组的正确形式填空，完成论文 Discussion 部分

> emerging　limitations　distinguish
> future studies　is associated with
> different type

（A）This paper is not without ＿（1）＿ and future work might well explore the following issues. First, we suggest that Foreign Direct Investment flowing to developed countries (such as the United States and the United Kingdom) may __(2)__ higher levels of reverse knowledge transfers than FDI to other __(3)__ countries. Second, we cannot __(4)__ strategic asset seeking FDI from other FDI motivations (e.g. natural resource seeking). __(5)__ might wish to examine the roles of __(6)__ of FDI in promoting innovation in host countries, and also to look at the impact of different entry modes.

| illustrate comparison shifting lead to |
| implication initial strong |

(B) Although this research's __(7)__ goal was the development of an Agri-fresh Food Supply Chain (AFSC) for perishable products, some managerial __(8)__ can be concluded from the results. The first practical insight refers to the __(9)__ of AFSC management to the location-inventory-routing AFSC management conceptually. The rest of managerial insight refers to the algorithms' dynamic sensitivity to find a well-tuned level of controlling parameters, as __(10)__ in Tables 2 and 3. This fact __(11)__ encourages further application and development of high-performance algorithms such as the proposed algorithm. Last but not least, the __(12)__ provided in Table 5 reveals that the location-inventory-routing model is efficient, __(13)__ a reduction in total distribution cost by 33% compared to the traditional supply chain.

练习2：阅读论文 "Nutrition Transition and Changing Food Preferences in India" (AE 14) 的 Limitations 部分，将下列引用与对应的信息功能配对

| 1. 介绍研究前景   2. 说明研究局限 |
| 3. 解释结果 |

(1) 功能：_____

- As highlighted by Strauss and Thomas (1995), expenditure survey data do not adequately control for food wastage.
- Smith (2015) raises a concern about the inadequacy of NSS in capturing consumption of meals consumed away from home, which leads to an underestimation of actual cereal consumption.

(2) 功能：_____

- As pointed out by Meenakshi (2016), because cereals have traditionally been consumed in large quantities, they are a major source of dietary iron. Therefore, there has been a decrease in aggregate iron intake by Indian households over time largely because of reduced cereal consumption.
- Indian households are unlikely to increase their food budget under the rising pressure of non-food expenses, as evidenced by the estimates of demand elasticities for food in this paper and the limited changes in real food expenditure observed by Deaton and Dreze (2009).

(3) 功能：_____

- As proposed by Narayanan and Gerber (2017) these results suggest a need to make existing policies such as the Public Distribution System more nutrition sensitive by widening the commodities being made available to the poor and marginalized.
- It has been argued by Kadiyala et al. (2014) that there is a need to refocus agricultural policy to better meet the changing nutritional needs of society.
- A useful extension of the current study would be to consider the rising consumption of processed food and beverages, another key feature of nutrition transition. These food items have become widely available in developing

countries because of globalization and the rise of supermarkets and fast food outlets (Reardon, 2015).

练习 3：将标号为 A~E 的句子填入 (1) ~ (5) 的位置，完成一个合理的论文结论（Conclusion）

_____(1)_____ Those concluding that finance is effective in reducing poverty and inequality have mainly focused on the dimension of financial deepening, concluding that it reduces income inequality and poverty in a linear fashion. Few have found an aggravating impact of financial development on the distribution of income, even though theory provides sound reasons why finance reduces inequality and poverty.

_____(2)_____ By testing 10 financial variables, we reveal that most of the financial development dimensions can help reduce income inequality and poverty. These dimensions include financial access, depth, efficiency, and stability. This paper also enriches the literature which studies the relationship between finance and income distribution.

_____(3)_____ In terms of the control variables, the findings also support the positive roles played by per capita income, government expenditure, and trade openness in reducing inequality and poverty. Inflation, however, is detrimental to income distribution.

In observing the benefits of financial development on both economic growth and income distribution, we conclude that policymakers need to steer the development of financial systems in pro-growth and pro-poor directions. _____(4)_____.

However, given that the development of a financial institution has a greater impact than the development of the stock market, officials may wish to give priority to banking sector improvement when considering the alleviation of poverty and income inequality. _____(5)_____.

Source: Financial development, inequality, and poverty: Some international evidence [J]. International Review of Economics & Finance[17]

A. Policymakers should encourage the creation of financial reform policies aimed at expanding financial access and depth, as well as enhancing financial efficiency and stability.

B. This paper has expanded the inquiry from financial depth to other dimensions of financial sector development: access, efficiency, stability, and liberalization, with a particular focus on income level and institution quality.

C. The effect of financial development on economic growth has been well documented in the literature using different econometric approaches and data samples.

D. Further research will focus on the policy settings and conditions in which financial Liberalization of banking sector could reduce poverty and income inequality.

E. However, among the five aspects tested in this paper, financial liberalization tends to have the opposite effect on inequality and poverty.

第 3 篇

SSCI论文辅体写作

第 9 章　标题与摘要

9.1　摘要的撰写

摘要是独立于论文主体，又体现主体内容"精华"部分的论文构成要素。当读者在电子资源的二次数据库（如 SSCI、A&HCI、Web of Science）中检索一篇论文时，可以找到论文的题目、摘要和关键词。对于带着某一研究兴趣、但需要在有限时间内进行海量搜索的读者来说，阅读一篇论文的"摘要"可以在最短时间内了解一项研究的主要活动、发现与意义，从而决定是否继续阅读论文的正文。

9.1.1　摘要的规范

以期刊《数学金融》（*Mathematical Finance*）为例，我们先来看一下期刊对投稿"摘要"的要求：

"A 100-200-word abstract communicating the essence of the paper is required. The abstract should succinctly and accurately describe the paper so that appropriate referees can be matched to the topic."[①]

通过上述描述可以总结期刊对"摘要"的要求如下：

（1）字数要求：一般在 100~300 之间；

（2）内容要求：简洁准确地描述论文内容；

（3）匹配要求：有助于审稿人将文章标题与内容相匹配。

9.1.2　摘要的信息要素

摘要是对论文的浓缩，其信息要素要与论文的结构和内容相对应。一般包含：研究背景（Background）（可选）、目的或活动（Purpose/Principle Activity）、方法（Method）、重要发现或结果［Result（s）］、主要结论和推论（Conclusion）（可选），示例见表 9-1~表 9-3。

例 9.1（AE 14）

（121 Words）

表 9-1　摘要示例

[1]We present empirical evidence on how changes in food preferences have contributed to nutrition transition, where the dietary pattern of households shifts away from traditional staples	P 目的
[2]Using household-level time series cross-section survey data for India, we estimate time varying demand elasticities, revealing evidence of the declining importance of cereals in Indian household diets	M+P 方法+主要活动
[3]The estimates show that Indian demand for cereals has become more income inelastic and price elastic. [4]We also find that cereals are a substitute rather than a complement to animal products in household diets. [5]Since changes in elasticities can only be attributed to variation in utility parameters, this indicates that cereals are losing favor with Indian households	R 结果
[6]These findings have implications for Indian food policy design and implementation	C 结论

[①] https：//onlinelibrary.wiley.com/page/journal/14679965/homepage/forauthors.html.

例 9.2 （AE 1） (162 words)

表 9-2 摘要示例

¹This study examines the effects of local and nationwide COVID-19 disease control measures on the health and economy of China's rural population	P 目的
²We conducted phone surveys with 726 randomly selected village informants across seven rural Chinese provinces in February 2020	M 研究方法
³Four villages (0.55%) reported infections, and none reported deaths. ⁴Disease control measures had been universally implemented in all sample villages. ⁵About 74% of informants reported that villagers with wage-earning jobs outside the village had stopped working due to workplace closures. ⁶A higher percentage of rural individuals could not work due to transportation, housing, and other constraints. ⁷Local governments had taken measures to reduce the impact of COVID-19. ⁸Although schools in all surveyed villages were closed, 71% of village informants reported that students were attending classes online	R 结果
⁹Overall, measures to control COVID-19 appear to have been successful in limiting disease transmission in rural communities outside the main epidemic area. ¹⁰Rural Chinese citizens, however, have experienced significant economic consequences from the disease control measures	C 结论

例 9.3 （AE 25） (85 words)

表 9-3 摘要示例

¹This paper aims to examine the relationship between political turnover and pollution discharges by listed firms in China	P 目的
²The empirical results show that political turnover is associated with more firm pollution discharges, particularly if the newly appointed officials are promoted locally or normally transferred. ³Furthermore, higher frequency of political turnover is linked with more pollution discharges. ⁴Lastly, our extended analysis illustrates that political connection is positively associated with firm pollution discharges and plays a moderating role in the relationship between political turnover and environmental performance	R 结果

例 9.3 展示一篇较为特殊的摘要——省略了背景、方法、结论等要素，将研究结果作为摘要主要内容。这种摘要适用于专业性较强的 SSCI 期刊论文，目标读者为该研究领域的资深研究者。

9.2 给论文一个"好"标题

SSCI 论文的标题是表达论文内容，反映研究范围和深度的最恰当、最简明的逻辑组合。其逻辑性体现在"以最少数量的单词来充分表述论文的内容"（Day[18]）。"好"标题首先有字数要求，以求简洁（brevity）。一般期刊要求 40~60 字符。此外，"好"标题还要实现准确（accuracy）和清楚（clarity）两个目标。例如，《数学金融》对论文标题要求为："A short informative title containing the major key words. The title should not contain Abbreviations"⊖。

上例说明投稿该期刊的论文应该有一个简洁但包含研究关键词的标题；并且标题中不应含有缩写。

⊖ https：//onlinelibrary.wiley.com/page/journal/14679965/homepage/forauthors.html.

《加拿大农业经济学报》(Canadian Journal of Agricultural Economics)期刊对论文标题要求描述如下①：
- A Running Head will be requested.
- It will give an accurate description of the main topic of the paper.

即投稿该期刊的论文应：
- 包含一个简洁版的论文标题。
- 标题应包含对论文主题的准确描述。

9.2.1 标题的基本功能

标题的作用主要体现在两方面：

1）便于文献检索。

图书馆和研究机构的数据库大都使用自动检索系统查找相关论文，其中有些是根据标题中的主题词来检索论文。因此，不恰当的标题很可能会导致论文"丢失"或产生漏检。

2）引起读者兴趣。

潜在读者在文献阅读和引用阶段需要处理大量信息，因而通常根据标题来考虑是否需要阅读摘要或全文。因此，即使论文被检索到了，如果标题不够清晰准确，也会失去潜在读者阅读和引用论文的机会。

9.2.2 标题的拟定及实例分析

在 Web of Science 中以"agriculture, economy"为关键词搜索 2014 年以来的高引论文（被引 300 次以上的 article，不包含 review），具体信息见表 9-4②。

表 9-4 "农业经济方向 SSCI 高引论文标题"示例

序号	论文标题	发表期刊	时间	被引	字数
标题 1	The role of biomass and bioenergy in a future bioeconomy: Policies and facts	Environmental Development	2015	352	13
标题 2	Global non-linear effect of temperature on economic production	Nature	2015	487	8
标题 3	Agriculture facilitated permanent human occupation of the Tibetan Plateau after 3600 B. P.	Science	2015	317	12
标题 4	How Circular is the Global Economy?: An Assessment of Material Flows, Waste Production, and Recycling in the European Union and the World in 2005	Journal of Industrial Ecology	2015	315	24
标题 5	Sixteen years of change in the global terrestrial human footprint and implications for biodiversity conservation	Nature Communications	2016	491	15
标题 6	Future urban land expansion and implications for global croplands	Proceedings of The National Academy of Sciences of USA	2017	308	9

我们可以对标题拟定的思路总结如下：

1. 描述变量或要素之间的相关性

此类标题为**关系导向型标题**——通过呈现变量或要素［如 A 和（或）B］对变量 C 在特定时间段或特定区域范围内的影响来呈现相关性。

（1）使用描述相关性的短语

标题 1：The role of biomass and bioenergy

---

① https://onlinelibrary.wiley.com/page/journal/17447976/homepage/forauthors.html.
② 被引次数以 Web of Science "所有数据库被引频次" 2021 年 8 月数据为准。

in a future bioeconomy: Policies and facts[19]

标题体现了"生物总量（biomass），生物能量（bioenergy）"这两个要素对"未来生态经济（future bioeconomy）"的影响。并使用短语"the role of..."直接表明。本文摘要对三者关系有如下描述：

> This paper provides a review of the policy framework for developing a bioeconomy in the European Union covering energy and climate, agriculture and forestry, industry and research. The Europe has a number of well-established traditional bio-based industries, ranging from agriculture, food, feed, fibre and forestbased industries. This paper proposes an analysis of the current status of bioeconomy in the European Union and worldwide until 2020 and beyond. We estimate the current bio economy marker at about: 24 billion, including agriculture, food and beverage, agroinclustrial products, fisheries and aquaculture, forestry, wood-based industry, biochemical, enzymes, biopharmaceutical, bioluels and bioenergy, using about 2 billion tonnes and employing 22 million persons. New sectors are emerging, such as biomaterials and green chemistry. The transition toward a bioeconomy will rely on the advancement in technology of a range of processes, on the achievement of a breakthrough in terms of technical performances and cost effectiveness and will depend on the availability of sustainable biomass.

标题 2：Global non-linear effect of temperature on economic production[20]

标题 2 体现了变量"温度（temperature）"对"经济生产（economic production）"在全球范围内产生的非线性影响，并使用短语"the effect of"直接表明。来看摘要中对研究结果部分的陈述：

> Here we unify these seemingly contradictory results by accounting for non-linearity at the macro scale. We show that overall economic productivity is non-linear in temperature for all countries, with productivity peaking at an annual average temperature of 13 degrees C and declining strongly at higher temperatures. The relationship is globally generalizable, unchanged since 1960, and apparent for agricultural and non-agricultural activity in both rich and poor countries.

（2）通过阐述应用来描述相关性

这类标题中一般含有"implications for…"等短语来说明在本研究中，变量的相关性重点体现在某方面的应用上。

标题 5：Sixteen years of change in the global terrestrial human footprint and implications for biodiversity conservation[21]

标题 5 介绍了从 1993 年至 2009 年共 16 年的时间段内，"全球陆地人类足迹（global terrestrial human footprint）"的变化及对"生物多样性保护（biodiversity conservation）"的影响。

> Here we use recently available data on infrastructure, land cover and human access into natural areas to construct a globally standardized measure of the cumulative human footprint on the terrestrial environment at 1km resolution from 1993 to 2009. We note that while the human population has increased by 23% and the world economy has grown 153%, the human footprint has increased by just 9%. Still, 75% the planet's land surface is experiencing measurable human pressures. Moreover, pressures are per-

versely intense, widespread and rapidly intensifying in places with high biodiversity. Encouragingly, we discover decreases in environmental pressures in the wealthiest countries and those with strong control of corruption.

标题 6：Future urban land expansion and implications for global croplands[22]

标题 6 体现了"未来城市用地扩张（future urban land expansion）"对"全球耕地（global croplands）"的影响。具体影响在摘要中描述得非常清楚。

Urban expansion often occurs on croplands. However, there is little scientific understanding of how global patterns of future urban expansion will affect the world's cultivated areas. Here, we combine spatially explicit projections of urban expansion with datasets on global croplands and crop yields. Our results show that urban expansion will result in a 1.8-2.4% loss of global croplands by 2030, with substantial regional disparities. About 80% of global cropland loss from urban expansion will take place in Asia and Africa. In both Asia and Africa, much of the cropland that will be lost is more than twice as productive as national averages. Asia will experience the highest absolute loss in cropland, whereas African countries will experience the highest percentage loss of cropland. Globally, the croplands that are likely to be lost were responsible for 3-4% of worldwide crop production in 2000. Urban expansion is expected to take place on cropland that is 1.77 times more productive than the global average.

（3）使用句子来描述相关性

标题 3：Agriculture facilitated permanent human occupation of the Tibetan Plateau after 3600 B.P.[23]

标题 3 中描述了"agriculture（农业）"对"permanent human occupation of the Tibetan Plateau after 3600 B.P.（校正后时间距今 3600 年的青藏高原永久性人类居住）"的影响，并通过动词"facilitate"指出这一影响是积极的。来看标题信息在摘要中的体现：

Using these data, we tested the hypothesis that a novel agro pastoral economy facilitated year-round living at higher altitudes since 3600 cal yr B.P. This successful subsistence strategy facilitated the adaptation of farmers-herders to the challenges of global temperature decline during the late Holocene.

2. 一定范围内的现状或变化趋势

此类标题为**结果导向型标题**——重点呈现某一变量或要素（如 A）的现存状态及在特定时间段或特定区域范围内的发展趋势。

标题 4：How Circular is the Global Economy? An Assessment of Material Flows, Waste Production, and Recycling in the European Union and the World in 2005[24]

标题 4 在"循环经济（Circular Economy）"背景下，呈现本研究的研究对象——"材料流动、废物生产与回收利用（material flows, waste production and recycling）"于 2005 年这一特定时间在欧盟及全球范围内的流通情况。

This article applies a sociometabolic approach to assess the circularity of global material flows. All societal material flows globally and in the European Union (EU-27) are traced from extraction to disposal and presented for main material groups for 2005. Our estimate shows that while globally roughly 4 gigatonnes per year (Gt/yr) of waste materials are recycled, this flow is of moderate size compared to 62Gt/yr of processed materials and outputs of 41Gt/yr. Our results indicate that strategies targeting the output side (end of pipe) are limited given present proportions of flows, whereas a shift to renewable energy, a significant reduction of societal stock growth, and decisive eco-design are required to advance toward a Circular Economy.

课外拓展与练习

★学术知识小课堂

写作中的泛指与特指——冠词"a/an/the"的使用

冠词（Article）是在英语中广泛使用的一类虚词，放在名词（短语）前用以说明该名词（短语）所指的信息。其类型包括：①不定冠词（Indefinite Article）——a/an；②定冠词（Definite Article）——the。

由于在汉语当中没有对应的冠词使用，母语为汉语的写作者往往因对冠词的使用不敏感导致使用错误，尤其是对定冠词"the"的不恰当使用。这些错误用法会引起读者对文中关键词的理解出现偏差，从而影响阅读效率和阅读体验。

对于冠词的正确使用，首先参考使用情景分类如图9-1所示。

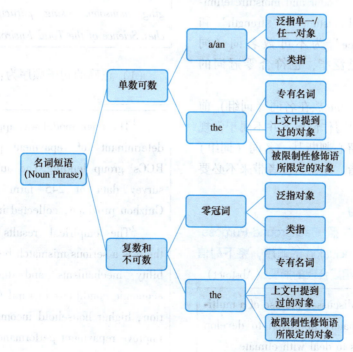

图9-1 冠词"a/an/the"的使用情景分类

接下来看具体的例子：

（1）<u>A</u> university is <u>an</u> institution of higher learning providing facilities for teaching and research and authorized to grant academic degrees①.

此句中,'university'和'institution'为单数可数,且这里是指任一所大学(泛指的任一对象),因此名词前使用了不定冠词 a/an(university 的首字母发/juː/音,而非元音,因此使用不定冠词 a;institution 的首字母发元音/i/,前面使用不定冠词 an)。

(2) Nanofabrics are textiles that are engineered with small particles that give ordinary materials advantageous properties such as water-proof, odor and moisture elimination, increased elasticity and strength, and bacterial resistance②.

此句中,'nanofabrics''textiles''small particles''ordinary materials'和'advantageous properties'为复数名词(词组),在这里都是泛指的概念,因此符合零冠词的情境;'water-proof''odor and moisture elimination''increased elasticity''strength'和'bacterial resistance'为不可数名词(词组),在这里也是泛指,也符合零冠词的情境。

综上,定冠词 the 放在名词(词组)前特指的情况在英语写作情境下并不属于常规做法。作者应该留心判断某一名词(词组)是否需要进行特指,以免给读者带来不必要的理解偏差。

★请完成以下练习

练习 1:请按照 Background-Purpose-Method-Result-Conclusion 的顺序,将下列信息进行重新排序,组成合理的摘要(Abstract)。

[1]This paper discusses the use of a multi-level and participatory approach to develop adaptation options to deal with climate related risks in a manner that contributes to stakeholder engagement, understanding of the risks, identification of the adaptation responses as well as its prioritization for risk reduction.

[2]Changes in rainfall patterns and temperatures are likely to affect water resources in India. [3] Also, changes in the extreme events will have direct implications on life and property.

[4]It highlights the importance of involving stakeholders from multiple levels as each level corresponds with different priorities in adaptation options.

Source:*Adaptation to changing water resource availability in Northern India with respect to Himalayan Glacier retreat and changing monsoons using participatory approaches. Science of the Total Environment*[25]

(1) 正确的句子顺序为:____—____—____—____。

[1]The Logit model was applied to test the determinants of repayment performance of RCCs' group lending. The authors used the survey data of 245 farm households in Guizhou province, collected in 2008.

[2]The empirical results indicate that there is a serious mismatch between joint liability mechanisms and the social and economic conditions in rural China. In addition, higher household incomes also did not improve repayment performance.

---

① https://www.merriam-webster.com/dictionary/university.

② https://patentanalysis.org/patent-analytics-report-nanofabrics/.

³This paper is an attempt to empirically explore the determinants of repayment performance in group lending programs in China. The results provide meaningful policy implications for the government and rural financial institutions.

⁴This paper aims to explore how borrower and group-level characteristics affect repayment decisions of group borrowers by highlighting the case of rural credit cooperatives (RCCs) in Guizhou province in Southwest China.

Source: *Determinants of repayment performance of group lending in China: Evidence from rural credit cooperatives' program in Guizhou province. China Agricultural Economic Review* [26]

(2) 正确的句子顺序为：____—____—____—____—____。

练习2：根据以下论文的摘要信息，补齐论文题目中所缺少的关键词

(1) 标题（Title）：Are _____ a problem across _____?

摘要提要（Abstract Excerpt）：Using the Bayley Scales of Infant and Toddler Development-Ⅲ（BSID-Ⅲ）, we examine the rates of developmental delays among children aged 0-3 years in four major subpopulations of rural China, which, altogether, account for 69% of China's rural children and 49% of children nationwide. With this large and broad sample, we show that, if China hopes to build up enough human capital to transition to a high-income economy, early childhood development in rural areas urgently requires more attention.

Source: *Are * * * a problem across * * *?. Journal of Comparative Economics* [27]

(2) 标题（Title）：The interface behavior between ____ and ____.

摘要提要（Abstract Excerpt）：In the present, studies of interaction between human normal flora and fibrous mineral are still lacking. Batch experiments were performed to deal with the interaction of Escherichia coli and two fibrous minerals (brucite and palygorskite), and the interface and liquid phase characteristics in the short-term interaction processes were discussed.

Source: *The interface * * * between * * * and * * *. Environmental Science and Pollution Research* [28]

练习3：请使用正确的冠词"a/an/the/*"，完成以下论文的摘要（Abstract）和数据收集（Data Source）部分

As ___(1)___ China has ___(2)___ important role in ___(3)___ global climate change, ___(4)___ Chinese government has set ___(5)___ goals to improve its environmental efficiency and performance and launched ___(6)___ carbon emission trading pilot markets in 2013, aiming to reduce ___(7)___ CO_2 emissions. Based on ___(8)___ panel data of 30 provinces from 2005 to 2017, this paper uses ___(9)___ difference-in-difference method to study ___(10)___ impact of China's carbon emission trading pilot markets on ___(11)___ carbon emissions and ___(12)___ regional green development. ___(13)___ paper also explores ___(14)___ possible influencing channels.

Source: *Examining the Impact and Influencing Channels of Carbon Emission Trading Pilot Markets in China. Sustainability*[29]

___(15)___ annual precipitation, ___(16)___ GDP, and ___(17)___ population data were derived from ___(18)___ resources and environment data center of ___(19)___ Chinese Academy of Sciences (http：//www. resdc. cn/). ___(20)___ D/data for ___(21)___ grain crop planted area and yield were derived from ___(22)___ Yunnan Statistical Yearbook and Sichuan Statistical Yearbook. ___(23)___ E/evation data were derived from ___(24)___ geospatial data cloud (http：//www. gscloud. cn) using ___(25)___ moving window method. All data were resampled to ___(26)___ 100 m grid for consistent analysis.

Source：*Multi-scenario simulation of ecosystem service value for optimization of land use in the Sichuan-Yunnan ecological barrier, China. Ecological Indicators*[30]

第 10 章　图表与表格

SSCI 论文的作者会使用**数据**（表格或图表）和**文本**两种形式来呈现研究结果。表格（table）和图表（figure）是"研究结果"的必要组成部分，它们是**精确呈现研究数据的视觉化形式**。在本章，我们就重点学习"研究结果"部分中"表格和图表"的运用。

10.1　图表与表格的信息要素

"图表（figure）"在 SSCI 论文中指的是图像（image）或图表（chart/graph）与说明性文字信息（figure legend[⊖]）的组合如图 10-1 所示。

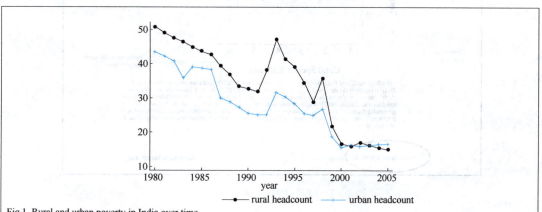

Fig.1. Rural and urban poverty in India over time.
This figure shows the trend in Rural and Urban Headcount rtatios in India. Rural and Urban Headcount ratios are the percentage of rural and urban population with monthly per capita expenditure less than the official poverty line respectively.The definitions and sources of all variables are in the Appendix table A1.

图 10-1　图表及其信息要素名称示例（AE 5）

在图 10-1 的示例中，我们看到这个图表包含了折线图及文字说明两个部分。除了原创的、高质量的图片或图形外，逻辑清晰、要素充分的"图表说明"也是非常必要的。一个好的"图表说明"应该包含以下要素：

1. 标题

图表标题是对图表信息的概括性介绍。标题的前面会有 Fig（ure）+序号的标识，如 Fig 2, Figure 3。由于图表说明的文字一般比正文文字的字号小，很多期刊要求图表标题以加粗的字体呈现，便于读者阅读。

标题的信息一般是介绍性的名词短语形式，表明所进行的研究的类型和内容。例如：

- **Decomposition of bank branches and total credit based on ownership** 基于所有权的商业银行分支机构及信贷总额分解
- The underlying logic linkages of the motivation, realization path, effects, spatio-

---

⊖　figure legend 也叫"图表说明"。

temporal changes, and risk evaluation of land finance 土地金融动机、实现路径、效果、时空变化和风险评估的内在逻辑联系。

2. 对图表中显著特征的描述

这部分信息包含对图表中所有的符号、形状、非标准化缩写、刻度条和错误条、标准偏差或标准错误的解释，以及任何其他潜在的非直观特征的介绍。

例如图 10-2 中，"Symbols are defined（符号的定义）"指示信息中，就指出"open triangles"（空心三角形）和"filled squares"（实心矩形）分别代表的变量。

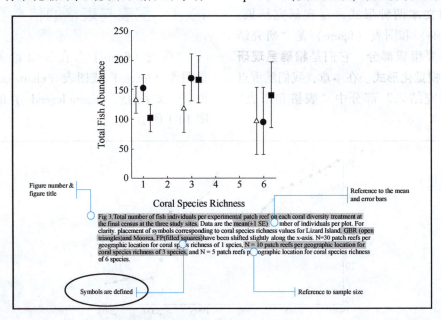

图 10-2　对图表中符号信息描述示例

10.2　图表与表格的描述

在对图表或表格进行文字描述时，作者一般不会简单地重复数据，因为这些数据是读者自己能够观察到的。作者一般会使用概括性语言通过比较、分析等方式将数据信息转换为文字版本。

来比较一下以下两个版本的描述如图 10-3 所示。

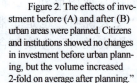

图 10-3　对论文中图表描述的文字比较

很显然，右侧方框中的语言通过对表格呈现信息的总结（The effects of investment before（A）and after（B）urban areas were planned）和对趋势变化的对比性描述（Citizens and institutions showed no changes in investment before urban planning, but the volume increased 2-fold on average after planning."），让读者更清晰地理解图表所要呈现的内容。

例

表 10-1 Knowledge and Practice of Public Smoking of College-Student Smokers

Statement	Y	N
Understanding of the harms of Public Smoking	85.4%	14.6%
Personal awareness of Non-Public Smoking Areas on campus	89.3%	10.7%
Personal awareness of Non-Public Smoking Areas outside of campus	80.4%	19.6%
Personal habit of not smoking in public areas	71.2%	28.8%
Strict PS prohibition on campus and in public	49.5%	50.5%
Inconvenience brought by the restrictions	78.0%	22.0%

表 10-1 呈现了"大学生烟民对公共区域吸烟的认知和实践"。以下版本（A）对表格的描述只是简单复述了表格中的内容，是不推荐的写法。

（A）

[1] Table 10-1 displays the percentage of college students' responses to their knowledge and practice of public smoking. [2] 85.4% claimed that they had a good understanding of the risks and disadvantages brought by public smoking; 89.3% and 80.4% were aware of Non-Public Smoking areas on and outside of campus. [3] 71.2% also claimed that they had personal habits of not smoking in public areas. [4] However, only 49.5% literally stuck to the rules of PS prohibition both on campus and in public. [5] 78.0% explained that the Non-smoking regulation brought inconvenience.

在论文写作中，对数据的呈现不能仅进行简单的陈列式描述，而要通过**概括、比较、解释说明**等方式体现。来看改进后的版本（B）：

（B）

[1] Table 10-1 displays the discrepancy between what the respondents claimed and what they actually practiced in terms of public smoking. [2] Although the majority reported a better understanding of the harms of public smoking（85.4%）and were aware of Non-Public Smoking areas both on campus and in public places（89.3% and 80.4% respectively）, only slightly over three-fourths of the respondents had personal habits of not smoking in public places. [3] Surprisingly, nearly half of them admitted that they did not strictly prohibit themselves from smoking in public areas. [4] This discrepancy may be due to inconvenience brought by the regulations as shown in question 5. The results agree with the studies of Marshall et al.（2018）.

课外拓展与练习

★ **学术知识小课堂**

在写作中描述变化趋势

在论文写作中，作者经常需要根据所呈现的图表和图形的变化来描述发展趋势。常用的表示变化的词组见表 10-2。

这些动词，以及相对应的名词，会搭配表示程度的副词或形容词使用以说明变化的幅度。具体可以分为：

（1）用"程度副词+动词"表示变化的幅度。

• The official indicators of overcapacity sectors fall sharply during this event.

（2）用"形容词+名词"表示变化的幅度。

表 10-2 描述变化的动词短语

图示	动词	图示	动词
↗	increase, grow	⋀	peak, reach the highest point
↘	decrease, decline, fall	↘	plummet, dip
2 → 4	double	∿	recover
4 → 2	halve	⋀⋁	fluctuate

- From 2013 to 2019, foreign direct investment to other Asian countries appears to reflect a <u>robust growth</u> in the Chinese economy, while the official unemployment rate displays <u>no variation</u>.

★请完成以下练习

练习1：请根据以下图表信息及方框中的词组完成图表描述

(A)
Table 1
Summary Statistics.

Variable	Explanation	Mean	Std.dev	Min	Max
Explained variable					
Technology Adoption Decision	1 = Adopted, 0 = Not adopted	0.671	0.469	0	1
Technology Adoption Degree	Technology adoption degree (%)	60.491	44.733	0	100
Adoption Time	Technology adoption Time (year)	6.369	9.356	0	41
Key explanatory variable					
Time preferences					
Discount rate	Discount rate of farmers	1.153	1.129	0	2.5
Scale	Actual farm size (acres)	59.048	212.270	0.3	5000
Control Variable					
Age	Age of household head (years)	57.635	10.226	27	87
Education	Education level of household head (years)	9.992	4.692	0	18

Source：AE 24

variables	average adoption time
accounting for	summary statistics
the sample	straw incorporation technology

Table 1 shows the ___(1)___ for the key ___(2)___ of interest from the household survey. Approximately 67.1% of the sample farmers adopted ___(3)___. The average proportion of adoption was 60.491%. The ___(4)___ was 6.369 years. Among the 1038 households, there were only 12 households with household heads aged under 35 years, ___(5)___ 1.16%. There were 621 households with household heads aged 55 and above (59.83%), indicating that ___(6)___ was mostly from elderly.

(B)

decline	recovery	well above
net negative	back up	dipped below
net positive	dipped precipitously	

Our Labor Market Conditions Index (LMCI) appears to capture the likely impact of key shocks on the Chinese labour market (Fig. 1). The index ___(7)___ 0 during the 2003-2004 period, suggesting that labour market sentiment was on ___(8)___. In the mid 2000s, the index was ___(9)___ 0 for several years, suggesting that labour market sentiment improved significantly and was on ___(10)___. The ___(11)___ in the index in 2007 was followed by a marked increase in 2008 reflecting employment gains which may be asso-

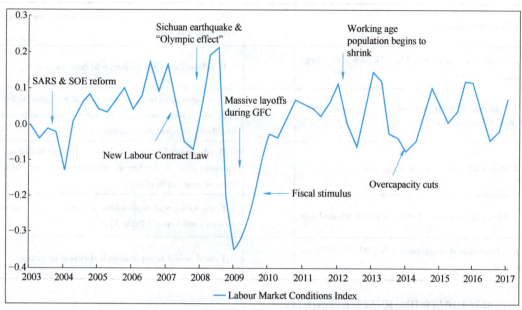

Source: Can media and text analytics provide insights into labour market conditions in China? *International Journal of Forecasting*, 35, (2019).

Fig. 1. Key historical shocks and the labour market conditions index in China

ciated with the reconstruction after the Sichuan earthquake and the 2008 Olympics. The index ___(12)___ during the global financial crisis (GFC) because of the significant employment loss over that period. It is estimated that around 23 million workers lost their jobs in China during the global financial crisis, as thousands of factories in the coastal region were closed as the number of orders filled by many export-oriented firms declined sharply (Cai & Chan, 2009).

Most these workers were migrants. The ___(13)___ in the labour market is reflected in the evolution of the LMCI which was ___(14)___ to 0 by mid-2010. From 2011 onwards, the LMCI suggests that sentiment in the Chinese labour market tended to be on net positive.

练习2：根据以下表格信息，将左右两列的信息进行配对，依据配对结果按序将字母编号填入空格中并完成图表描述的写作

TABLE 3　Reported changes in employment

Interview questions	Result
Villagers unable to work because workplaces are closed	539/726 (74.24%)
Villagers unable to use public transportation to travel to the city	593/726 (81.68%)
Villagers unable to drive or carpool to the city	467/726 (64.32%)
Villagers unable to rent a place to stay in the city	680/726 (93.66%)
Villager decided not to leave the village to work due to fear of infection	487/726 (67.08%)

Note. Data are n/N(%), where N is the total number of village informants who responded to each question.

Source: AE 1

1. The survey revealed	A. villagers with wage-earning jobs outside the village were unable to work
2. Nearly three quarters (539, 74.24%) of village informants reported that	B. villagers were not permitted to drive themselves
3. Four out of every five village informants (593, 81.68%) reported that	C. villagers were not permitted to rent any place to live in a city, given restrictions by urban governments and neighborhood community leaders
4. Most (467, 64.32%) reported that	D. villagers did not want to leave the village to find employment even if the hiring, transportation, and rental barriers were not in effect
5. Almost all informants (680, 93.66%) reported that	E. the widespread implications of disease control measures on employment (Table 3)
6. A large share of village informants (487, 67.08%) reported that	F. local public transportation had ceased operating

请根据上述信息用一段话描述表格内容：

第 4 篇

SSCI论文投稿与发表

第 11 章 期刊选择与论文投稿

当你需要了解论文的投稿与发表环节，这意味着你可能已完成自己的论文初稿（paper draft/manuscript）。祝贺你取得的进展！但需要提醒的是，从完成论文初稿到论文的发表可能需要很长一段时间，这个过程对于新手研究者来说往往要持续数月甚至数年。

论文的投稿与发表过程其实就是一场竞赛。你与若干个不相识的竞争对手同场竞技，接受期刊审稿人统一参考标准下的评价，以"投稿被最终接受"为赢得竞赛的标准。想要成为这场比赛的赢家，你需要了解投稿的几个基本要点（Cargill & O'Cornoll[7]）。

- 认真选择目标期刊，按照期刊要求从格式和内容上优化你的初稿；
- 站在同行专家和期刊编审的立场审视初稿，给你的论文一个合理的框架，并清晰描述研究创新点和贡献；
- 在投稿前，邀请有经验的同行对你的初稿进行预审；
- 认真对待期刊反馈的审稿意见，向编审充分展示你在审稿意见指导下如何改进论文。

11.1 选择目标期刊

在第 2 章介绍过，SSCI 收录期刊目录中，单经济管理类的期刊就有 857 种[注]，每种期刊都关注特定的研究领域并有特定的投稿要求。如何在众多期刊中选择适合发表自己文章的期刊呢？

11.1.1 利用题目与关键词筛选期刊

（1）将拟发表的论文手稿题目中包含的关键名词和论文摘要部分的关键词提取出来。

（2）选择数据库（如 Google Scholar，Web of Science，Elsevier 等），使用数据库的"高级检索（Advanced Search）"功能键入关键词，检索最近 3~5 年内发表的相关文章。

（3）将检索到的文章制作一个"目标期刊列表"。

11.1.2 阅读"作者指南"

SSCI 收录的每种期刊都有自己的网站并对期刊进行详细的介绍，其中包含本刊独有的"作者指南"。制作好"目标期刊列表"后，登录列表中的期刊网站，阅读期刊简介。对于感兴趣的期刊，认真阅读其"投稿指南"。在阅读时，应着重了解期刊的以下几个方面。

（1）期刊目标与投稿范围（Aims and Scope）

"目标与范围"这个栏目简要介绍本期刊收录论文的类型，研究领域和收录要求。投稿人可以从这里初步了解自己的研究是否契合该刊的发表需求。

例 11.1

> The Journal of Development Economics publishes original research papers relating

---

[注] 此分类依据 JCR 学科分区，截至 2021 年 6 月 30 日数据。

> to all aspects of economic development - from immediate policy concerns to structural problems of underdevelopment. The emphasis is on quantitative or analytical work, which is novel and relevant. The Journal does not publish book reviews. We welcome papers that take up questions in development economics that are of interest to the general readers of the journal, and then use data from a particular country or region to answer them. However, we do not publish articles that are essentially in-depth studies of a specific country, region, case, or event whose findings are unlikely to be of great interest to the general readers of the journal⊖.

在以上来自《发展经济学学报》（*Journal of Development Economics*）期刊"目标与范围"的描述中，清晰地说明了本刊的投稿范围和要求——"发表与经济发展相关的原创研究，不发表书评"。并且说明"论文要能够回答该期刊普通读者感兴趣的问题，然后利用特定国家或地区的数据来回答这些问题。"然而，不会发表那些"本质上是只针对某个特定国家、地区、案例或事件的深入研究的文章，因为这些研究的发现不太可能引起普通读者的兴趣"。

（2）期刊编委会（Editorial Board）

编委会通常由主编（editor in chief）、副主编和若干编辑委员⊖组成。编委会成员大多为该出版物所属学科的专家学者以及这个领域的权威人士。了解编委会成员的组成，也是了解目标期刊的收录范围和研究兴趣的重要方式。

（3）摘要与索引（Abstracting and Indexing）

这部分主要介绍收录本刊的数据库信息及期刊的影响因子等信息。

以《发展经济学学报》期刊为例，在"Abstracting and indexing"页面可以看到收录该期刊的数据库信息，从图11-1的标记可以看出该期刊是一份 SSCI 收录期刊。

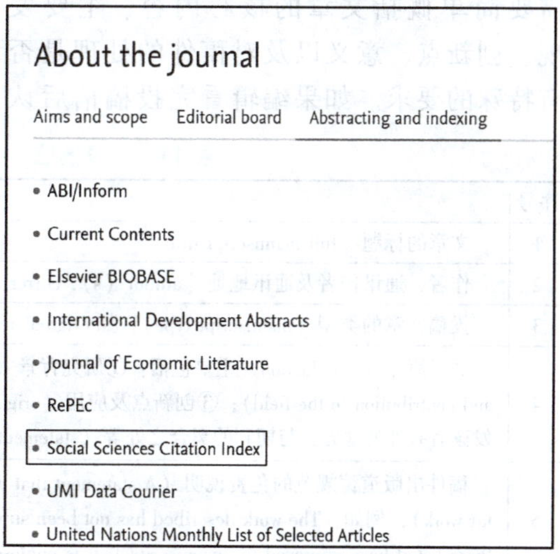

图 11-1　期刊"摘要与索引"示例
（*Journal of Development Economics*）

11.1.3　阅读"投稿指南与要求"

每份 SSCI 期刊对本刊发表文章的内容和格式都有统一的要求，这些要求都会写入本刊的"投稿指南与要求（submission guidelines and requirements）"中，向投稿人介绍投稿的格式，引用规范，出版费用及其他要求等。期刊网站上都有详细的引导来帮助作者完成投稿的相应步骤。

⊖ https://journals.elsevier.com/journal-of-development-economics.

⊖ 副主编的英文表达尚无统一说法。在多数 SSCI 期刊中，编委会成员还有 co-editor（联合编辑）、associate editor（副编辑）和 information editor（责任编辑）等。

11.2 撰写投稿信

在首次提交论文时，一些期刊会要求作者一并提交投稿信（cover letter）。投稿信的目的是让期刊编辑在阅读你的论文之前，可以快速了解文章的基本内容及特殊要求。投稿信是编辑对论文的第一印象，需要简单概括文章的核心内容、主要发现、创新点、意义以及对稿件的处理是否有特殊的要求。如果编辑看完投稿信后认为你的研究不符合期刊目的和范围，或者不具备创新点及意义，可能就不会去阅读你的论文。因此投稿信是初步判断你的论文是否可以进入期刊评议环节的重要依据，必须认真撰写。

有的期刊会要求在投稿信中附上主要作者的通信信息，有的期刊还会要求推荐审稿人。具体要求要在期刊的"作者指南"中查阅。如果没有具体说明，就按照通用的要求写作。

投稿信的信息要素见表 11-1。

表 11-1 投稿信（cover letter）的信息要素

序号	要素名称
1	文章的标题（full manuscript title）
2	作者、通讯作者及通讯地址 [author(s), corresponding author and contacts]
3	投稿文章的类型（manuscript type），如 original research/review/book review 等
4	文章简介（introduction）主要包括：①研究背景（research background）；②论文的重要发现及贡献（main findings and contribution to the field）；③创新点及应用（originality and implications）；④论文可以发表在本期刊上的原因：引发读者兴趣的地方，与期刊的契合之处等（statements of why the manuscript is appropriate for the target journal）
5	稿件出版道德规范的免责说明（A statement that there is no multiple or redundant publication of the same or very similar work），例如：The work described has not been submitted elsewhere for publication, in whole or in part, and all the authors listed have approved the manuscript that is enclosed
6	稿件出版利益冲突的免责声明（A statement that there is no potential conflict of interest such as financial interest）
7	推荐审稿人和/或屏蔽竞争对手成为审稿人 [Suggestions of potential reviewers to include and/or some individuals to be excluded from peer review（explaining why）] 请求屏蔽某人，例如：Due to a direct competition and conflict of interest, we request that Dr. XXX of *** University not be considered as reviewer 推荐审稿人，例如：The following is a list of possible reviewers for your consideration： ① Name A E-mail：××××@××××；② Name B E-mail：××××@××××

例 11.2

Cover Letter & Declaration Form

Date：May 21, 20**

Submission Title：**

Type of submission：original research

Author(s)：AA, BB, CC

Corresponding author：AA

Contact e-mail：sadeghi98@yahoo.com

Dear Editor,

As a corresponding author, I declare that the paper "***" submitted for publication in the Journal of *** is my original research work. It does not infringe any personal or property rights of another. The work does not contain anything libelous or otherwise illegal.

I confess that the work contains no material from other works protected by copyright that have been used without the written consent of the copyright owner, or that I can provide copies of all such required written consents to journal upon request.

I have properly cited the works of others in the text as well as in the reference list. I further declare that the manuscript submitted for publication has not been previously published and is not currently under review elsewhere.

The novelty of my work lies in working on the recently-published textbooks based on CLT method where there are few research studies due to their new publication.

I hereby warrant that I am submitting my original work, that I have the rights in the work, that I am submitting the work for first publication in the Journal and that it is not being considered for publication elsewhere and has not already been published elsewhere, and that I (We) have obtained and can supply all necessary permissions for the reproduction of any copyright works not owned by me.

Sincerely Yours,

Agreed & Accepted by

AA (Corresponding Author)

11.3 准备初稿

1. 准备匿名手稿

匿名手稿（anonymous manuscript）指不包含任何指向作者信息的论文初稿。其要点就是审稿人不能够通过阅读论文初稿来确定作者，从而对论文质量和价值做出公正、诚实的判断。

有些期刊采用"双向匿名（double/mutual-anonymous）"评审系统，即作者与审稿人互相不知道对方的真实身份信息。

例 11.3

NAIS Journal's Author Guidelines for Making a Manuscript Anonymous

An anonymous manuscript does not contain author name (s) in: the manuscript, any in-text citations, the reference list, or in the properties section of the Word document. Please provide us with a manuscript that follows these directions; if you do not know how to remove your name from the properties of your document, please let us know and the Managing Editors can help you. When you submit your manuscript, submit a separate Microsoft Word file that includes the author (s) bio sketch and contact information.

上例中，《美国土著研究》（*Native American and Indigenous Studies*）期刊对如何准备匿名手稿进行了简要介绍——匿名手稿在以下部分不允许出现作者姓名及个人信息，包括正文、文本引用、引用列表或 Word 文档的"属性"部分。并告知作者，如果不知道怎么从文档的属性中删除本人信息，可以联系本刊责任编辑完成匿名。在提交手稿时，作者需要提交一个单独的包含作者身份信息和联系方式的 Word 文档。

2. 整理附录及其他信息

（1）附录（Appendix）放在正文后面，包含不适合放在正文中的额外信息。例如，在 APA 格式论文中，附录（Appendix）是放在参考书目（Reference List）之后如图 11-2 所示。

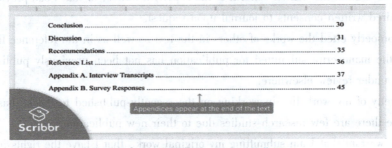

图 11-2　附录（Appendix）的位置

此外，作者还要关注期刊对附录部分的格式要求，按照要求准备附录的内容。

图 11-3 所示为 APA 中附录的格式要求。

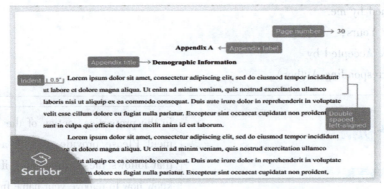

图 11-3　APA 中附录（Appendix）的格式要求示例

（图片来源：https://www.scribbr.com/apa-style/appendices/）

（2）附加材料（Supplementary Materials）

根据论文数据量及期刊版面要求，将在正文中展示不了的辅助性的数据及图片等放在"附加材料"部分对文章结果进行支撑。一般期刊会提供"附加材料"的专有链接，以供对本文感兴趣的读者进一步获取资料。

显示作者身份相关信息的稿件。这些可能出现作者身份信息的部分包括正文、文内引用、参考文献及 Word 文档的属性部分。这些相关信息需要在提交论文时在另一个单独的 Word 文档中包含。

一般情况下，默认为是论文作者负责在向期刊提交手稿前将所有可能让审稿人知道他（们）身份及所在机构的信息遮盖掉。

二、为什么匿名投稿很重要

匿名稿件的核心就是不让审稿人知道作者信息，有助于审稿人在审阅稿件时做出公正的判断。

课外拓展与练习

★ 学术知识小课堂
　　如何匿名你的投稿
　　一、什么是匿名稿件

匿名稿件（anonymous manuscript）是指在投稿资料中去掉了论文作者名称及能够

三、匿名作者相关信息的技巧

（1）隐藏具体位置及机构信息——利用"文字搜索"在论文中找到包含"位置及学校机构"的信息，如果有，按照下面的方式进行匿名。例如：

× These data were collected from incoming master's level students at the School of Social Studies, Southwestern Technical University.

√ Data were collected from first-year social work students enrolled in a graduate-level program at a university in Southwest China.

√ Data were collected from first-year students enrolled in the SDS program at [location masked for anonymous review].

（2）隐藏机构审查委员会声明中的大学机构名称——遮盖声明中的大学名称时，写出大学所在区域即可。例如：

× This research was approved by the "Southwestern Technical University Institutional Review Board."

√ This research was approved by the Institutional Review Board of a national university in Southwest China.

（3）隐藏作者对已发表研究的自我引用——在"文内引用"和"参考文献"中，作者在自引时用"Author"替换自己的名字。例如：

× In our investigation of Miao language, we found that there has been drastic decline of fluent speakers in the 1990s.（Author）

√ Scholarship on the Miao language has found a drastic decline of fluent speakers in the 1990s（Author）.

并在参考文献处，作者用以下方式进行匿名：

References

√ Author. [masked for anonymous review]

Source：NAIS journal Author Guidelines for Making a Manuscript Anonymous.①

---

① https：//www.naisa.org/wp-content/uploads/2020/09/How-to-Make-a-Manuscript-Anonymous.

第 12 章 论文的修改与发表

12.1 SSCI 论文的"同行评议"制度

12.1.1 "同行评议"制度起源

早在 1665 年,时任英国皇家学会秘书之一的亨利·奥尔登堡(Henry Oldenburg)(1618—1677)出资印刷并发行刊物《皇家学会哲学会刊》(The Philosophical Transactions of the Royal Society)(以下简称《哲学会刊》)。在编辑这份刊物的时候,亨利提前将组好的稿件交给这一领域的专家学者进行评审并提出意见,这开创了在学术期刊领域引入同行评价方式的先例。《哲学会刊》成为首部采用同行评议程序出版和发行的期刊,因此也被认为是全世界第一本真正意义上的学术期刊。自此之后,"同行评议"就成为科学交流的正式组成部分。

维基百科对"同行评议(Peer Review)"的定义如下[①]:

"the evaluation of work by one or more people with similar competencies as the producers of the work (peers). It functions as a form of self-regulation by qualified members of a profession within the relevant field."

可见"同行评议"过程是一篇论文获得同一领域中专家认可的过程。为了保证期刊的影响力和文章的质量,影响因子越高的期刊越倾向采用更严格的同行评议过程来筛选发表在本刊的论文。

12.1.2 期刊编辑与审稿人

确定了目标期刊,将论文初稿提交(submit your manuscript)后,谁是论文初稿的第一读者呢?先来认识一下以下两个角色:

1. 期刊编辑(Journal Editor)

与作者及审稿人联系。负责审阅来稿的投稿信(cover letter)及论文初稿(manuscript),以确定稿件是否符合期刊目标,是否能进入"同行评议"环节。

2. 审稿人(Reviewer/Referee)

某一研究领域内具有学术权威及发表经验的专家学者。负责对期刊编辑指定的论文来稿进行写作质量、创新性等方面的评价。

这两类人群就是一篇论文初稿的第一读者。其中,审稿人对于论文的评审起着关键作用。一般会由 2~3 位审稿人共同评审同一篇初稿。虽然作为一个独立研究者,每位审稿人的视角和立场不同,但有一些共性的评审标准是每位审稿人都需考虑的。具体的共性评价标准见表 12-1。

表 12-1 "期刊审稿人评审标准"示例

Reviewer's Evaluation Criteria		
1. Originality 原创性	Does the paper contain new and significant information adequate to justify publication?	○ Yes ○ No

---

① https://en.wikipedia.org/wiki/Peer_review.

(续)

2. Relationship to Literature 文献的引用	Does the paper demonstrate an adequate understanding of the relevant literature in the field and cite an appropriate range of literature sources?	○ Yes ○ No
	Is any significant work ignored?	○ Yes ○ No
3. Methodology 恰当的方法	Is the paper's argument built on an appropriate base of theory, concepts, or other ideas?	○ Yes ○ No
	Has the research or equivalent intellectual work on which the paper is based been well designed?	○ Yes ○ No
	Are the methods employed appropriate?	○ Yes ○ No
4. Results 可靠的结果	Are results presented clearly and analyzed appropriately?	○ Yes ○ No
	Do the conclusions adequately tie together the other elements of the paper?	○ Yes ○ No
5. Implications 研究的意义及前景	Does the paper identify clearly any implications for research, practice and/or society?	○ Yes ○ No
	Does the paper bridge the gap between theory and practice?	○ Yes ○ No
	Can the research be used in practice (economic and commercial impact), in teaching, to influence public policy, in research (contributing to the body of knowledge)?	○ Yes ○ No
	Are these implications consistent with the findings and conclusions of the paper?	○ Yes ○ No
6. Quality of Communication 写作质量	Does the paper clearly express its case, measured against the technical language of the field and the expected knowledge of the journal's readership?	○ Yes ○ No
	Has attention been paid to the clarity of expression and readability, such as sentence structure, jargon use, acronyms, etc.?	○ Yes ○ No

12.2 投稿的反馈

绝大部分论文投稿后都要经历修改才能被期刊正式接收。在评议完初稿后,审稿人会应期刊编辑要求对论文"是否推荐收录至本期刊"进行结果评价。期刊编辑会将审稿人的意见反馈给作者,反馈意见分为以下三种情况:

1. 重大修改(Major Revision)

"重大修改"指审稿人对文章的研究主题感兴趣,但认为论文还没有满足表 12-1 中列出的某一大类或某几大类标准,要求论文作者针对这些标准对论文进行修改。我们先通过例 12.1 和例 12.2 来看一看期刊编辑或审稿人如何表述"重大修改"的信息。

例 12.1

Request for Major Revision

Dear Dr. ***,

Thank you for submitting your manuscript to International Journal of F***.

I have completed my evaluation of your manuscript. One Associate Editor also looked at the manuscript and provided me with an assessment, based on reviewers' reports.

The Associate Editor and I recommend reconsideration of your manuscript after a major revision. This means that, while we feel that the work presented in the manuscript might be of interest for the journal, re-submitting your manuscript does not necessarily mean it will be accepted, eventually.

When revising your manuscript, please consider all issues mentioned in the reviewers' reports carefully. Please outline in a cover letter every change made in response to their comments and provide suitable rebuttals for any comments not addressed. Please resubmit your revised manuscript by Aug 27, 20**.

To submit your revised manuscript, please log in as an author at https://www.editorialmanager.com/***/, and navigate to the "Submissions Needing Revision" folder.

International Journal of F*** values your contribution and I look forward to receiving your revised manuscript.

例 12.2

Request for Major Revision

Dear ***,

Thank you for submitting your manuscript to Journal of I*** E***.

Based on the attached, I regret to inform you that your manuscript entitled ***, cannot be accepted for publication in its present form.

You may revise your manuscript according to the reviewer comments and re-submit it for a second review round along with a statement mentioning the way you have dealt with the reviewer comments; note that you may not comply with some reviewer comments but you must address all reviewer comments in your statement.

被要求进行"重大修改"一般意味着这篇论文将会在修改后重新进入"同行评议"环节。在第二轮评审中，审稿人会被问到"你是否认为本文作者根据第一轮评审结果对他们的文章进行了必要的修改，这样的稿件现在是否可以接受发表"等类似的问题。因此在邮件中，编辑或审稿人都会要求作者对审稿人提出的修改意见进行一对一的回应。

2. 小范围修改与临时接受（Minor revision and provisional accept）

"小范围修改"是一篇投稿收到的比较积极的审稿回复，这意味着审稿人对论文的研究问题和内容比较满意，仅对论文的一些细节，如数据处理方式、格式、语言等方面的呈现提出修改意见，以使论文达到收录出版标准。"暂时接受"意味着经过同行评审，投稿论文已被暂定为接受并等待发表。不过，在编辑把投稿论文交给出版部门之前，期刊的编辑团队会认真核对检查投稿论文是否具备发表的一切条件。

例 12.3

Minor Revision and Provisional Accept

Dear Dr. ***,

I am pleased to confirm that your paper entitled "***" will be accepted for publication in S*** if you consult an English editing service (such as those listed on our website), because the paper would greatly benefit from some strong editing.

Also, check the formatting of citations and references- there are some articles available for free download on our website.

Please therefore find a right person to do these corrections, and send back the manuscript highlighting the corresponding changes made.

Thank you for considering *** as a venue for your work. I hope we will receive a revised submission soon so we can proceed with what looks like an interest research topic.

Regards,

"小范围修改与临时接受"也有可能出现在"重大修改"之后。经过第二轮评审，审稿人对作者的修改结果表示满意，并同意在"小范围修改"基础上接受论文并发表。

例 12.4

Minor Revision and Provisional Accept

Dear Dr. ***,

Thank you for submitting your manuscript to International Journal of F***. It is a pleasure to accept it in its current form for publication.

Our comments (Associate Editor and myself), and any reviewer comments, are gathered below.

Your accepted manuscript will now be transferred to our production department. We will create a proof which you will be asked to check, and you will also be asked to complete a number of online forms required for publication. If we need additional information from you during the production process, we will contact you directly.

We appreciate and value your contribution to International Journal of F***. We regularly invite authors of recently published manuscript to participate in the peer review process. If you were not already part of the journal's reviewer pool, you have now been added to it. We look forward to your continued participation in our journal, and we hope you will consider us again for future submissions.

Kind regards,
Prof. P***P**
Editor-in-Chief
International Journal of F***

Editor and Associate Editor comments:
Reviewer 1: Thanks for answering the questions I had. I have no further suggestions or comments.
Reviewer 2: My previous recommendation was "minor revisions" based on some remarks. All these remarks have been addressed, so I recommend the acceptance of the paper.
Reviewer 3: This version represents an improvement compared to the original one.

The authors satisfactorily addressed the technical suggestions made in my last review.

There is only one point of concern: the maintenance of Gender and Ethnicity as explanatory variables. I know that they may be proxies for a series of omitted (not available) variables, but I think the cautionary note made on lines 319-25 of page 21, is not enough to avoid the encouragement the use of these variables in credit scoring models - what, potentially, may be used to discriminate social groups. My suggestions are:

a) remove these variables from the models or

b) adjust the manuscript text by naming them as var1 and var2, mentioning they are borrower specific characteristics that cannot be disclosed.

A minor suggestion: if this paper is accepted, Appendix A may be removed from the text and be available electronically.

3. 拒绝与重新投稿（Rejection and Resubmission）

如果投稿论文的写作质量不高或研究主题不符合目标期刊要求，会被直接拒稿。如果来稿被拒，编辑会在邮件一开始就直接告知此信息，并解释原因。

例 12.5

Rejection Letter

Dear Dr. ***,

I am writing in regard to manuscript titled "***" which you submitted to the Journal of ***.

Based on my own reading and reviewers' comments enclosed at the bottom of the mail,

I regret not being able to recommend publication of your manuscript.

Containing no innovate ideas, this manuscript is extremely long and obscure to read. Besides, the research questions discussed in the writing are not of interest to the prospective readers of this journal.

We know that this may come as a disappointment, but hope you can use the reviews to improve the paper.

Kindly regards,

当然，还有一种情况是本次来稿被拒绝，但是如果进行重大修改，可以重新投稿。这种情况下，编辑一般会附审稿人的修改意见。来看下面的例子：

例 12.6（Part I）

Rejection and Resubmission

Dear ***,

Thank you for submitting your manuscript to A*** E***. I regret to inform you that your paper is not acceptable for publication. We have completed the review of your manuscript and a summary is appended below. The reviewers have advised against publication of your manuscript and I must therefore reject it at this time. For your information and guidance, any specific comments explaining why I have reached this decision and those received from reviewers, if available, are listed at the end of this letter.

You have the option of resubmitting a substantially revised version of your paper, which would be considered as a new submission. If you decide to do this, you should refer to the reference number of the current paper and include a cover letter which explains in detail how the paper has been changed or not, in reply to the Editor and Reviewer comments.

Thank you for giving us the opportunity to consider your work.

Kind regards,

在邮件后半部分,编辑附上了审稿人意见,主要内容如下:

例12.6(Part Ⅱ)

Comments From The Editors and Reviewers

-Reviewer 1

This paper proposes * * * . The authors claim that experiment results show that * * model yields more promising results than other * * * algorithms in terms of accuracy and adaptation ability to varying working conditions. The research issue is interesting, and the paper is well organized and written in general. Some of my suggestions are mentioned in below.

1. This paper focuses on * * * . However, this topic has been discussed for many years. The innovation and value of this research should be strengthened.

2. The abstract only illustrates the concept of research and does not summarize the core values ?? and quantitative benefits of proposed * * * model.

3. In the related works section, the authors only briefly explain each * * * .

4. In Fig. 4, the functions of each component should be described in detail, especially in * * * .

-Reviewer 2

Based on the following comments, this paper is not ready for publication.

My major concern is that this paper does not fit to the scope of the journal. What is the contribution to the advanced development economics?

Some sections are too long. Consider to make it concise. For Introduction, consider it move some sentences to Literature Review.

The contribution of the article (in the context of * * and * *) should be highlighted more in Introduction.

How SDAE [24], ML-TEM [29] and BPNN were selected for the comparison? Need a justification.

从上述审稿人意见可以看出,审稿人1对于这篇投稿的内容较为认可并提出了一些修改意见,而审稿人2建议直接拒绝这份投稿。如果作者想要进行重大修改并重新投稿,必须按照审稿人的意见逐条进行修改,并认真思考如何能够回答审稿人2的意见以改变其对稿件的看法。

12.3 论文的修改与回复

12.3.1 撰写回复信

只要投稿没有被直接拒稿,对于作者来说就是好消息。作者应积极并认真对照审稿人提出的修改的意见,逐条对论文进行修改。在重新提交时,要附上回复信(response letter)说明在文中是怎样进行修改的。

回复信的内容一般分为两部分:

一是致谢编辑及审稿人的修改意见（例 12.7 Part Ⅰ）；

二是说明按照审稿人意见逐一对论文的修改（例 12.7 Part Ⅱ）。

例 12.7（Part Ⅰ）

> **Response Letter**
>
> Dear Editor and Referees,
>
> We appreciate the opportunity to revise this paper (Paper ID：＊＊＊). We thank the referees for their careful and insightful review of our manuscript and for providing constructive comments and thoughtful suggestions. Based on these comments and suggestions, we have provided further clarifications and made careful modifications to the original manuscript. These suggestions have helped us to improve the paper. Our responses to your specific informative comments are below. For your convenience, we have replicated your comments (in italics) with our replies inserted below.

12.3.2　呈现论文的修改

在收到带有审稿人意见的邮件后，作者需要根据意见对手稿进行修改（revision）。这种修改是对审稿意见的逐一回复并指出每一条意见的修改在修改后的手稿（revised manuscript）中的位置。在进行逐条回复时，可采取列表型回复和文字型回复，列表型回复见表 12-2。

（1）格式一：列表型回复

例 12.7（Part Ⅱ）

表 12-2　邮件中对审稿人意见逐一回复

Comment Type/Number	(Author) Response	Where in Manuscript
1. On page 5, line 17： I suggest to include, in beginning of section 4, the USD equivalent to CNY 57Bi and CNY 26K in terms of 2019 exchange rate.	We have converted the Chinese Yuan (CNY) to US Dollar (USD) using the exchange rate on 31 December 2019 (i.e. 1 CNY = 0.143 USD) and provided USD equivalent values in the revised draft	Page 5, Section 4, line 18
2. Introduction： (1.1) Page 1, line 48-49： Provide a recent reference to support the affirmation："is now widely considered as one of the most important innovations in development policies．．．．"	We added two more recent studies, Cull & Morduch (2017) and Fan et al. (2019), to support the affirmation. References： (1) Fan, Y., John, K., Liu, H. &Tamanni, L. (2019). Security design, incentives, and Islamic microfinance: Cross country evidence. Journal of International Financial Markets, Institutions and Money, 62, 264-280. (2) Cull, R. & Morduch J. (2017). Microfinance and economic development. Handbook of finance and development, Edward Elgar Publishing, Cheltenham, UK	page 1, section 1.1, line 49
3. (2.2) Page 5, lines 48-55： Can you add anything about the advantages/disadvantages of NLA comparing to MCMC methods in terms of the quality of the outcomes?	we added that INLA is "a deterministic algorithm that provides accurate and fast Bayesian inference and is described in the following section."	page 5, section 2.2, line 53-55

（2）格式二：文字型回复

例 12.8

Response to Referee 2

Referee 2's comment:

"I find the paper ' * * * ' well written, significant and interesting. I acknowledge that I am not an expert on random effects, so I trust the paper's model and empirical results based on Journal editors' experience. I have some minor remarks."

Response:

First of all, we would like to thank you for your positive comments. We will respond to your comments point-by-point below.

1. Page 3, second paragraph, third line: change "fist" to "first"

Response:

Thank you for pointing this typo out, we changed it.

2.1.5) Page 3, lines 17-29: Justify why you chose the cited models. What are their advantages in comparison with other options?

Response:

Thank you for your comments. In the introduction, we mentioned that "We choose these models because they are widely used in the literature on spatial statistics (Banerjee et al., 2014)." We explained in detail the main reasons why we choose these models in Section 3.1. The first specification with independent random effects is in line with Sohn and Kim (2007). The second specification

---

represents a conditionally autoregressive (CAR) model and we explained "We choose a CAR model because it is computationally very convenient to estimate complicated joint statistical relationships using a set of conditional dependencies (Banerjiee et al., 2014)." We also explained that the third specification proposed by Leroux et al. (2000) "it represents a weighted average of the first two specifications considered in this paper" (page 6).

12.4　论文的制作与发表

每份期刊在内容呈现时都有本刊统一标准。一篇论文被期刊接收后，还要接受期刊制作部门（production department）一系列的编辑和制作才能正式发表。例如，编辑会逐条检查并更正"文献综述"部分的引用是否与文中一一对应，对文中的专有名词进行核实等。

对于母语不是英语的作者来说，改进语言也是论文制作中的重要环节。大的出版商会提供语言编辑服务——将论文手稿交由母语人士编辑或专业的语言编辑团队进行处理。例如 Springer 就有两个附属机构"自然研究编辑服务（Nature Research Editing Service）"[①] 和"美国期刊专家（American Journal Experts）"[②] 为作者提供医学、生命科学、化学、物理、工程、商业、经济和人文科学方向论文的语言服务。如果没有，论文制作团队也会在编辑过程中向作者指出需要修改的语言问题。

[①] https://authorservices.springernature.com/language-editing/.

[②] https://www.aje.com/.

下面，我们以学术期刊出版商 Wiley 的 "Production Process" 为例，来展示论文制作过程和出版商向作者提供的服务，如图 12-1 所示。

六步发表你的论文 Six steps to publish your paper					
论文接收 Article accepted	文案排版 Copyediting and typesetting	校对更正 Proofing and corrections	提前查看发表 Earlyview publication	网络发布 Issue published online	访问共享 Access and sharing

图 12-1 "论文发表过程"示例（Wiley）

1. 论文接收

（1）通讯作者会收到期刊发送的一封电子邮件，要求其登录或注册作者服务（Author Service），并确保文章已添加到"我的信息显示板（My Dashboard）"。此时，请导航到"修改我的详细信息（Amend My Details）"页面，选择是否：

- 使用 Wiley 的混合公开访问选项（如果期刊不是完全公开访问）发布文章。
- 为您的文章签署许可协议（a license agreement）。
- 跟踪文章的发布状态（请求在论文制作的每个阶段接收电子邮件提醒）。
- 将您的作者服务帐户与您的 ORCID⊖关联。

（2）有些期刊为"已接收文章（Accepted Article）"[也称"已接受版本（Accepted Version）"]提供在线发表（online publication）。文章被接收后，只要作者同意期刊的"接收文章条款及条件（Accepted Version Terms and Conditions）"，文章立即在网上发布，可以被下载及引用。

2. 文案排版

期刊编辑团队会从写作风格、语法和术语命名等方面对您的文章进行文案编辑并进行排版，使文章的标准达到您的研究所应有的水平。

3. 校对更正

（1）校对。在编辑排版后，文章又会返回作者手中，在最后发表前让作者对文章进行再次审阅。文章校对的链接会通过电子邮件发送。请准确校对您的文章，并清楚标记需要更正的地方。

（2）已处理更正。您的更正将被接收并处理。

4. 提前查看发表

（1）提前查看*（有在线版本）的文章会在正式出版前在 Wiley 在线图书馆（Wiley Online Library）发表。您现在可以在线查看已发表的文章。

（2）此时起，您的文章不会再做任何改动。

（3）访问在线 PDF 会被看作是电子打印稿或 PDF 打印稿。

（4）你的提前查看文章包含一个在线出版日期和引用 DOI，可以完整被引。

（5）您现在可以生成一个共享链接来共享您的文章。

5. 网络发布

（1）包含您文章的一期期刊内容可以在网上找到。

⊖ ORCID：（Open Researcher and Contributor ID），即开放研究者与贡献者身份识别码。拥有 ORCID 识别码的学术研究者可以将识别码添加到期刊文章的作者姓名中，保证其工作不与同名者混淆。ORCID 的支持者包括所有主要的科技出版商，包括 Elsevier、Wiley、Nature、Thomsen Reuters 等。

(2) 印刷版本可能在网络发行之前或之后。

6. 访问共享

当您的文章在网上发表后：

(1) 您将收到电子邮件提醒（如果需要）。

(2) 作为作者，您可以（在接受使用条款和条件后）自由查看您的文章。

(3) 您可以使用 Author Services 信息板上的"共享文章（Share Article）"按钮生成一个独特的共享链接，将您的文章的全文、只读版本进行无限共享。

(4) 您可以订购您的文章再版（reprints）；再版指南/示会在校对阶段发送给投稿期刊。

(5) 如果需要更改作者列表，请填写"作者信息更正申请表（Authorship Change Form）"，联系编委会及论文制作办公室来完成你的请求⊖。

⊖ 只有部分期刊提供此项服务。

附录 示范论文(Article Examples)列表

AE 1: Health, economic, and social implications of COVID-19 for China's rural population. Agricultural Economics, 2021, Volume 52(3): 495-504. https://doi.org/10.1111/agec.12630.

AE 2: Eco-innovation and its role for performance improvement among Chinese small and medium-sized manufacturing enterprises. International Journal of Production Economics, 2021, Volume 231, 107869, ISSN 0925-5273, https://doi.org/10.1016/j.ijpe.2020.107869.

AE 3: Policy assessments for the carbon emission flows and sustainability of Bitcoin blockchain operation in China. Nature Communications, 2021, Volume 12, 1938, https://doi.org/10.1038/s41467-021-22256-3.

AE 4: The role of China's aid and ODI in the economic growth of African countries. Emerging Markets Review, 2020, Volume 44, 100713, https://doi.org/10.1016/j.ememar.2020.100713.

AE 5: Finance, law and poverty: Evidence from India. Journal of Corporate Finance, 2020, Volume 60, 101515, https://doi.org/10.1016/j.jcorpfin.2019.101515.

AE 6: When a son is born: The impact of fertility patterns on family finance in rural China. China Economic Review, 2014, Volume 30: 192-208, https://doi.org/10.1016/j.chieco.2014.06.008.

AE 7: A benchmark of machine learning approaches for credit score prediction, Expert Systems with Applications, 2021, Volume 165, 113986, ISSN 0957-4174, https://doi.org/10.1016/j.eswa.2020.113986.

AE 8: Heterogeneous choice in the demand for agriculture credit in China: results from an in-the-field choice experiment. China Agricultural Economic Review, 2021, Volume 13, No. 2: 456-474. https://doi.org/10.1108/CAER-06-2020-0151.

AE 9: Spatio-temporal variances and risk evaluation of land finance in China at the provincial level from 1998 to 2017. Land Use Policy, 2020, Volume 99, 104804, ISSN 0264-8377, https://doi.org/10.1016/j.landusepol.2020.104804.

AE 10: Analysis of spatial variability in factors contributing to vegetation restoration in Yan'an, China. Ecological Indicators, 2020, Volume 113, 106278, https://doi.org/10.1016/j.ecolind.2020.106278.

AE 11: Assessing China's efforts to pursue the 1.5℃ warming limit. Science. 2021, Volume 372: 378-385. DOI: 10.1126/science.aba8767.

AE 12: The China Shock: Learning from Labor-Market Adjustment to Large Changes in Trade. Annual Review of Economics, 2016, Volume 8: 205-240, https://doi.org/10.1146/annurev-economics-080315-015041.

AE 13: Risk Aversion and Son Preference: Experimental Evidence from Chinese Twin Parents. Management Science, 2017, Volume 64, No. 8: 3469-3970. http://doi.org/10.1287/mnsc.2017.2779.

AE 14: Nutrition Transition and Changing Food Preferences in India. Journal of Agricultural Economics, 2020, Volume 71: 118-143, https://doi.org/10.1111/1477-9552.12322

AE 15: Friends with benefits: Patronage networks and distributive politics in China, Journal of Public Economics, 2020, Volume 184, 104143, https://doi.org/10.1016/j.jpubeco.2020.104143.

AE 16: Banking credit worthiness: Evaluating the complex relationships, Omega, 2019, Volume 83: 26-38, ISSN 0305-0483, https://doi.org/10.1016/j.omega.2018.02.001.

AE 17: Spatial Effects of Air Pollution on Public Health in China. Environment and Resource Economics, 2019, Volume, 73: 229-250. https://doi.org/10.1007/s10640-018-0258-4.

AE 18: Can information influence the social insurance participation decision of China's rural migrants? Journal of Development Economics, 2021, Volume 150, 102645; https://doi.org/10.1016/j.jdeveco.2021.102645.

AE 19: Finance and Growth for Microenterprises: Evidence from Rural China. World Development, 2015, Volume, 67: 38-56, ISSN 0305-750X, https://doi.org/10.1016/j.worlddev.2014.10.008.

AE 20: Rollover Risk and Credit Risk. The Journal of Finance, 2012, Volume 67: 391-430. https://doi.org/10.1111/j.1540-6261.2012.01721.x.

AE 21: Eco-innovation and its role for performance improvement among Chinese small and medium-sized manufacturing enterprises, International Journal of Production Economics, 2021, Volume 231, 107869, https://doi.org/10.1016/j.ijpe.2020.107869.

AE 22: A credit rating model of microfinance based on fuzzy cluster analysis and fuzzy pattern recognition: Empirical evidence from Chinese 2,157 small private businesses. Journal of Intelligent & Fuzzy Systems, 2016, Volume 31(6): 3095-3102. https://doi.org/10.3233/JIFS-169195.

AE 23: How productive is public investment? Evidence from formal and informal production in India. Journal of Development Economics, 2021, Volume 151, 102625, https://doi.org/10.1016/j.jdeveco.2021.102625.

AE 24: Time Preferences and green agricultural technology adoption: Field evidence from rice farmers in China. Land Use Policy, 2021, Volume 109, 105627, https://doi.org/10.1016/j.landusepol.2021.105627.

AE 25: Political turnover and firm pollution discharges: An empirical study. China Economic Review, 2019, Volume 58, 101363, https://doi.org/10.1016/j.chieco.2019.101363.

部分参考答案

第 2 章 参考答案

练习 1：

1. （1）primary （2）secondary
2. （1）secondary （2）primary
3. （1）secondary （2）primary

第 3 章 参考答案

练习 1：

（2）distribution：the act of giving or delivering something to a number of people. 分配

（1）

词 汇	含 义	结 构	其他常用形式
standardization	标准化	standardize+（a）tion	standard, standardize
quantitative	量化的	quanti+（a）tive	quantify, quantity
qualitative	质性的	qualit+（a）tive	qualify, disqualification
negative	（数）负的；消极的；否定的；（电）阴性的	neg+（a）tive	negate, negation
normalization	常态化；正规化	normalis+（a）tion	abnormal, enormous
technique	技巧；技术；手法	techn（o）+ique	biotechnics, architect
transform	改变，使…变形；转换	trans+form	transact, translate uniform, conformity

（3）discrete：independent of other things of the same type. 离散（的）

（4）approximate：（v.）to be similar or close to something in amount, quality 近似为

（5）layer：a level or part within an organization, a society or a set of idea（组织内）层次

练习 2：

（2）

词 汇	含 义	结 构	其他常用形式
strategic	战略的	strato+（e）gic	strategy, stratography
anticipatory	预期的；提早发生的	anti+cip+atory	anticipate, anticipation
sustainability	持续性；永续性	sus+tain+abl（e）+ility	abstain, contain, success
underlying	adj. 潜在的；根本的；v. 放在…的下面；为…的基础	under+ly（lie）+ing	undergo, underestimate
geographical	地理上的	geo+graph+ic（al）	geology, autograph, biography
network	网络，系统	net+work	Internet, intranet, netted

练习 3：

（1）The Texas High Plains（THP）is a productive agricultural region, and it relies heavily on the exhaustible Ogallala Aquifer for irrigation water for crop production.

（2）①At both locations, treatments were

organized as a split-block design and four replications (were) conducted.

②At both locations, treatments were organized as a split-block design with a four-time replication/four replications.

(3) There is substantial heterogeneity in wealth, access to credit from the formal sector and family functioning across regions in China.

(4) A common explanation for distributive favoritism is a form of collective corruption, whereby clients help their patrons steal the money from public coffers.

(5) Attributes are product characteristics influencing consumer choice among different items.

练习4:

(1) an annual addition/aggregation

(2) stress response and mechanism regulation (s)

(3) Incidence rate of over-expenditure or Over-expenditure incidence rate

(4) Research model uncertainties

(5) the variation coefficient weighing of the 19 indices

第4章 参考答案

练习1:

(1) 4—1—3—2

(2) 3—4—2—1

(3) 2—1—3

练习2:

1—c 2—d 3—a 4—f 5—b 6—e

第5章 参考答案

练习1:

(1) 2 (2) 1 (3) 4 (4) 3

练习2:

(A)

(1) have agreed (2) have focused

(3) began (4) using

(5) is (6) may be

(7) release (8) to be released

(B)

(1) began (2) launched

(3) had included (4) retook

(5) pushing (6) had averaged

(7) growing (8) highlight

练习3:

(1) The aim of this study was to identify the (possible) influences of agricultural soil management on soil microbiological composition and abundance.

(2) This study seeks to determine which farmer characteristics and what contextual environmental factors will lead to good or bad credit for farmers.

第6章 参考答案

练习1:

(1) 3. 介绍使用该方法的目的

(2) 4. 描述研究对象特征

(3) 5. 描述研究过程

(4) 2. 给出是否选择一种方法的理由

(5) 1. 描述标准的或之前使用过的方法

练习2:

(1) The aim (2) using

(3) provided by (4) According to

(5) are shown (6) Since

(7) In particular (8) Finally

第7章 参考答案

练习2:

(1) 3. 对研究结果进行总结

(2) 4. 通过表格或图表说明研究结果

(3) 2. 对研究结果进行评价

(4) 1. 解释结果出现的意外和偏差

练习3:

(1) Fig. 3a shows that access to informal and formal financial services is also important for the size of the initial investment for the microenterprises.

(2) It can be observed in Fig. 3d that the coefficients of shares of meals consumed outside the home are significant and negative.

(3) Columns (1) and (2) give the preference-based elasticities, which are computed using the mean data point in 2017-2018.

(4) As seen from Figs. 2 and 3, Moran's I increased from 0.231 to 0.277 during 2004-2013, which indicates that the local autocorrelation of Y1_ RT had been enhanced in China.

(5) In comparison with the estimated results in Table 2, we can see that the negative effect of PM2.5 concentration on public health was higher than that without considering the spatial factor.

练习 4:

(1) additionally (to introduce a new fact or argument)

(2) arbitrarily (not based on any principle, plan or system)

(3) not surprisingly (parenthesis, to show expected finding)

(4) effectively (in a way that produces the intended result)

第 8 章　参考答案

练习 1:

(1) limitations
(2) be associated with
(3) emerging
(4) distinguish
(5) Future studies
(6) different types
(7) initial
(8) implications
(9) shifting
(10) illustrated
(11) strongly
(12) comparison
(13) leading to

练习 2:

(1) 2　　(2) 1　　(3) 3

练习 3:

(1) C　　(2) B　　(3) E
(4) A　　(5) D

第 9 章　参考答案

练习 1:

(1) 正确的句子顺序为：2—3—1—4
(2) 正确的句子顺序为：4—1—2—3

练习 2:

(1) Are infant/toddler developmental delays a problem across rural China ?

(2) The interface interaction behavior between E. coli and two kinds of fibrous minerals

练习 3:

(1) *　　(2) an　　(3) *
(4) the　(5) *　　(6) *
(7) *　　(8) *　　(9) the
(10) the　(11) *　　(12) *
(13) The　(14) *　　(15) *
(16) *　　(17) *　　(18) the
(19) the　(20) *　　(21) *
(22) the　(23) *　　(24) a
(25) a/the (26) a

第 10 章　参考答案

练习 1:

(1) summary statistics
(2) variables
(3) straw incorporation technology
(4) average adoption time
(5) accounting for
(6) the sample
(7) dipped below
(8) net negative
(9) well above
(10) net positive
(11) decline
(12) dipped precipitously
(13) recovery

(14) back up

练习2：

1. E 2. A 3. F 4. B 5. C 6. D

参考例文：

The survey revealed the widespread implications of disease control measures on employment (Table 3). Nearly three quarters (539, 74.24%) of village informants reported that villagers with wage-earning jobs outside the village were unable to work because their workplaces were closed due to the COVID-19 outbreak. Four out of every five village informants (593, 81.68%) reported that local public transportation had ceased operating, and most (467, 64.32%) stated that villagers were not permitted to drive themselves.

Almost all informants (680, 93.66%) indicated that rural individuals were not permitted to rent any place to live in a city, given restrictions by urban governments and neighborhood community leaders. A large share of village informants (487, 67.08%) stated that the fear of infection was so great that villagers did not want to leave the village to find employment even if the hiring, transportation, and rental barriers were not in effect.

参考文献
REFERENCES

[1] DUAN H, WANG S, YANG C. Coronavirus: limit short-term economic damage [J]. Nature, 2020, 578 (77-96): 515.

[2] ALTMAN E I. Financial ratios, Discriminant analysis and the prediction of corporate bankruptcy [J]. The Journal of Finance, 1968, 23: 589-609.

[3] HOLLAND H. Adaptation in Natural and Artificial Systems: an introductory analysis with applications to biology, control and artificial intelligence [M]. Boston: MIT Press, 1992.

[4] SHI B, CHEN N, WANG J. A credit rating model of microfinance based on fuzzy cluster analysis and fuzzy pattern recognition: empirical evidence from Chinese 2,157 small private businesses [J]. Journal of Intelligent & Fuzzy Systems, 2016, 31 (6): 3095-3102.

[5] BRIANE G. Writing in the natural sciences and engineering. In Belcher D., Braine G. (eds.) Academic Writing in a Second Language: Essays on Research and Pedagogy [M]. New Jersey: Ablex, 1995.

[6] WEISSBERG R, BUKER S. Writing up research: experimental research report writing for students of english [M]. New Jersey: Prentice Hall, 1991.

[7] CARGILL M, O'CONNOR P. Writing scientific articles: strategy and steps (second edition) [M]. Oxford: Wiley-Blackwell, 2013.

[8] LEWIS M. The Lexical Approach: The State of ELT and a way Forward (Vol. 1, p. 993) [M]. Hampshire: CENAGE, 1993.

[9] 蔡基刚. 国际SCI期刊论文写作与发表 [M]. 上海: 复旦大学出版社, 2020.

[10] 俞炳丰. 科技英语论文实用写作指南 [M]. 2版. 西安: 西安交通大学出版社, 2011.

[11] 钱颖一. 理解现代经济学 [J]. 财经科学, 2002, S1: 1-8.

[12] 陈强. 计量经济学及Stata应用 [M]. 北京: 高等教育出版社, 2015.

[13] SMALLBONE T, QUINTON S. Increasing business students 'confidence in questioning the validity and reliability of their research [J]. Electronic Journal of Business Research Methods 2004, 2 (2): 153-162.

[14] HEALE R, TWYCROSS A. Validity and reliability in quantitative studies [J]. Evidence-based nursing, 2015, 18 (3): 66-67.

[15] DROST E A. Validity and reliability in social science research [J]. Education Research and Perspectives. 2011, 38: 105-124.

[16] 朱会. 基于主成分分析法的职业经理人创新能力提升影响因素分析 [J]. 科技管理研究, 2018, 38 (9): 134-138.

[17] ZHANG R, NACEUR S B. Financial development, inequality, and poverty: Some international evidence [J]. International Review of Economics & Finance, 2019, 61: 1-16.

[18] DAY R A. How to write and publish a scientific paper (5th ed.) [M]. Phoenix: The Oryx Press, 1998.

[19] SCARLAT N, DALLEMAND J, MONFORTI-FERRARIO F, et al. The role of biomass and bioenergy in a future bioeconomy: Policies and facts [J], Environmental Development, 2015, 15: 3-34.

[20] BURKE M, HSIANG S, MIGUEL E. Global non-linear effect of temperature on economic production [J].

Nature, 2015, 527: 235-239.

[21] VENTER O, SANDERSON E, MAGRACH A, et al. Sixteen years of change in the global terrestrial human footprint and implications for biodiversity conservation [J]. Nature Communications, 2016, 7: 1-11.

[22] D'AMOUR C B, REITSMA F, BAIOCCHI G, et al. Future urban land expansion and implications for global croplands [J]. Proceedings of the National Academy of Sciences, 2016, 114 (34): 8939-8944.

[23] CHEN F H, DONG G H, ZHANG D J, et al. Agriculture facilitated permanent human occupation of the Tibetan Plateau after 3600 B. P. [J]. Science, 2015, 347 (6219): 248-250.

[24] HAAS W, KRAUSMANN F, WIEDENHOFER D, et al. How circular is the global economy? An assessment of material flows, waste production, and recycling in the European Union and the world in 2005 [J]. Journal of industrial ecology, 2015, 19 (5): 765-777.

[25] BHADWAL S, GROOT A, BALAKRISHNAN S, et al. Adaptation to changing water resource availability in Northern India with respect to Himalayan Glacier retreat and changing monsoons using participatory approaches [J]. Science of the Total Environment, 2013, 468-469: S152-S161.

[26] ZHANG Q, IZUMIDA Y. Determinants of repayment performance of group lending in China: Evidence from rural credit cooperatives' program in Guizhou province [J]. China Agricultural Economic Review, 2013.

[27] WANG L, LIANG W, ZHANG S, et al. Are infant/toddler developmental delays a problem across rural China? [J]. Journal of Comparative Economics, 2019, 47 (2): 458-469.

[28] DAI Q, HAN L, DENG J, et al. The interface interaction behavior between E. coli and two kinds of fibrous minerals [J]. Environmental Science and Pollution Research, 2018, 25 (23): 22420-22428.

[29] WU Q, TAMBUNLERTCHAI K, PORNCHAIWISESKUL P. Examining the impact and influencing channels of carbon emission trading pilot markets in China [J]. Sustainability, 2021, 13 (10): 5664.

[30] LI C, WU Y, GAO B, et al. Multi-scenario simulation of ecosystem service value for optimization of land use in the Sichuan-Yunnan ecological barrier, China [J]. Ecological Indicators, 2021, 132: 108328.